THE BATTLE FOR TWELVELAND

By the same author

Fiction

THE FRAT WAGON
JOURNEY TO NO END
THE MIGHTY FALLEN
LEST I FALL

Military History

DECISION AT ST VITH
PATTON—A CRITICAL BIOGRAPHY
FORTY-EIGHT HOURS TO HAMMELBURG
MASSACRE AT MALMEDY
WEREWOLF
FINALE AT FLENSBURG
HUNTERS FROM THE SKY

Linguistics

SPIEGE GESPRÄCHTE
a textbook for interpreters

The Battle for Twelveland

AN ACCOUNT OF ANGLO-AMERICAN
INTELLIGENCE OPERATIONS
WITHIN NAZI GERMANY 1939–1945

by

Charles Whiting

LEO COOPER · LONDON

First published in Great Britain 1975 by
Leo Cooper Ltd, 196 Shaftesbury Avenue, London WC2

Copyright © Charles Whiting 1975

ISBN 0 85052 180 7

Printed in Great Britain by
Western Printing Services Ltd, Bristol

'*This was a secret war whose battles were lost or won unknown to the public . . . no such battle has ever been waged by mortal man.*'

CHURCHILL

'*The tales and descriptions of that time without exception speak only of self-sacrifice, patriotic devotion, despair, grief—heroism. But it was not really so . . . Most of the people at that time paid no attention to the general progress of events, but were guided only by their private interests.*'

TOLSTOY

'*Zwoelfland, Zwoelfland Über Alles.*'

DRUNKEN ABWEHR OFFICERS,
ISTANBUL *1943*

CONTENTS

ILLUSTRATIONS

ACKNOWLEDGEMENTS

I should like to thank the following people for their kind assistance:

BRITAIN: Professor R. Jones, David Irving, Group-Captain F. Winter-botham, Sir Kenneth Strong, Field-Marshal Sir Gerald Templer, Patrick Seale, Professor Sir Hugh Trevor-Roper, A. Denniston.

GERMANY: Economics Minister Dr Friderichs, Dipl. Ing. Albert Speer, Colonel Giskes, Colonel and Frau N. Ritter, Heinz Hoehne (*Spiegel*), Jochen von Lang (*Stern*), Dr G. Deschner (*Die Welt*), Dr K. Simon (*Aachener Volkszeitung*), Direktor Carl Wiberg, D. Hespers, Frau L. Heydrich, Dr Sareyko (*Auswaertiges Amt*), Peter Norden, W. Ertz.

HOLLAND: Wolfgang Trees.

LUXEMBOURG: M. Henri Koch, Directeur Leon Nilles (*Revue*).

UNITED STATES: Tom Stubbs, David Khan, Major 'F'.

INTRODUCTION

One of the last major gaps in our knowledge of the Second
World War concerns the role played by the Anglo-American
intelligence services—the 'eyes and ears' of their respective
governments—*within* National Socialist Germany. We have
a fairly comprehensive knowledge of the various resistance
and emigré espionage organizations in the occupied countries
and the work of such units as the SOE.[1] But the members
of these organizations were amateurs and the agents on the
ground often lacked central direction and control. But what
of the first team—the professionals?

Unfortunately, those professionals, whose code-name for
Germany was 'Twelveland', hence the title of this book,
are not prepared to talk about their activities in Germany
during the war. Today any researcher attempting to find out
about the British Secret Intelligence Service and its associate,
the US Office of Strategic Services, meets the same barrier of
silence that the enemy—Admiral Canaris' *Abwehr*—must
have encountered over thirty years ago.

Both General Sir Kenneth Strong and Admiral Sir
Norman Denning, wartime Intelligence men and post-war
heads of Intelligence, preferred not to recollect anything 'at
this distance in time' when approached. Field-Marshal Sir
Gerald Templer, the last head of the SOE's German section,
'could not imagine' who could assist the researcher, and
hadn't the 'vaguest idea who might help'. Sir Hugh Tevor-
Roper, Regius Professor of Modern History at Oxford and
wartime SIS man, was even more to the point: 'I do not
know whether we had any personal sources within Germany
and I, myself, would not have believed anything they said
anyway!' And this from the man whose task it was to study
the rival service, the *Abwehr*. But it was left to 'Zero C',
Group-Captain Winterbotham, for sixteen years a member

[1] The British Special Operations Executive.

of the secret organization located in the shabby rabbit-warren that was the SIS headquarters opposite St James's Park underground station, to lay it on the line: 'I fear you won't get very far with your research . . . there is an absolute ban on SIS operations in World War II being published!'

This hardcast reticence about the role intelligence played in the war in the shadows against Nazi Germany is understandable. It goes without saying that a secret service wants to remain secret, for who can tell when information long thought useless can be used again.[2] But there is another reason. Too many Germans who worked for the SIS and OSS hold, or have held, important positions in both the German Democratic Republic and the Federal Republic. Thus the last conservative government in West Germany could boast a minister who had spied for both the Russians and the French[3] and a secretary-of-state who had been secretly employed by the British. Its socialist successor can claim a minister who was sentenced to prison for spying for the Russians and who is suspected of then transferring his services to the SIS. Indeed its erstwhile leader, Chancellor Willy Brandt, employed as his chief adviser a man who went to jail as a Soviet spy and ten years later was sentenced to death as an OSS spy!

And those Germans in prominent positions who spied for the Western Allies (and they are not all in the Federal Republic) are not all politicians; they are found in every walk of life: education, diplomacy, big business, the police and especially the security services.[4]

There are, therefore, good reasons why the SIS and the now defunct OSS do not want the story of their wartime exploits in Germany published. Yet if one searches hard

[2] My Czech informant, Major 'F', who worked for Czech intelligence for seventeen years after the war, said that his service keeps comprehensive files on leading politicians' wartime records, which were used against them if necessary.

[3] Unwittingly he also served the SIS, but he went to his grave not knowing that.

[4] The writer must point out, however, that he is deeply grateful to one of those security services for informing him—just in time—that he was *persona non grata* on the other side of the Iron Curtain. How their agents knew, I didn't ask; and I don't think they would have told me even if I had.

enough one can find witnesses to this strange drama played off-stage: the dutch grocer who saw Schellenberg and his thugs crash across the border at Venlo and capture the two chiefs of the Continental SIS in 1939; the *Abwehr* man who drugged a British SIS agent in the Hotel Vier Jahreszeiten in Hamburg in 1940 to check whether he was genuine or not; the old Luxembourg railwayman who treasured his son's letters from Peenemuende in 1942 which finally made clear to the SIS in London that the Germans had perfected the V-2; the Belgian farmer's wife who remembers the OSS smuggling their agents through her Ardennes farmyard and across the border into Germany; and the Eifel village boy who recalls those same agents being beaten to death by enraged villagers in 1944.

All the manifold aspects of this strange and tortuous story are there still, in spite of London's prohibitions; for in the end the decisions made by 'C', the remote head of the SIS, in his fourth-floor office in the Broadway Building, and 'agent 110', or 'Mr Bull' as he was sometimes codenamed, at Number 23 Herrengasse, Berne, could only result in violence and victims.

It is a story which should be told. In a well-ordered society, its security service must protect the members of that society from their own innocence, blindness—even stupidity. In the Second World War the SIS and the OSS did not always do that. Between 1939 and 1945 the British Service was an archaism in many ways, artificially protected against necessary change. Its American counterpart, the OSS, which it had helped to create, learned its trade from the wrong people—the bumbling *Abwehr* operators who could not resist meddling in politics; and General Schellenberg's intellectual thugs with their liking for mayhem and murder. The blunders of the OSS's direct successor, the Central Intelligence Agency, in countries ranging from Vietnam to Venezuela have shown us just how fatal those early lessons were.

Yet, in spite of the two services' shortcomings, their achievements in the war were tremendous. Not only did the

British outwit their enemies, the *Abwehr*, they also tricked their erstwhile ally, Russia. The Americans, for their part, brought off the great coup of infiltrating agents into virtually every section of German life and finally brought about the surrender of a great German army. But even these achievements paled before the British operation which allowed its leaders to know in advance virtually every move of the German High Command for four years. The real battle for Twelveland was not won in the shadowy backstreets of Hamburg and Berlin by sinister Allied spies. It was won by elderly Oxford dons in a rusty tin hut in the middle of the home counties.

Book One

The Battle Begins

'I can't tell you what sort (of job) it would be.
All I can say is that if you join us you mustn't
be afraid of forgery and you mustn't be afraid
of murder.'

*SIS recruiting officer to
Colonel Sweet-Escott, London 1940*

PART ONE

CLASH IN THE SHADOWS

(1939–40)

'The British Secret Service has a great tradition. Germany possesses nothing comparable to it. Therefore each success means the building up of such a tradition and requires even greater determination. The traitors who would stab Germany in the back during this most decisive struggle must be ruthlessly destroyed. The cunning and perfidy of the British Secret Service is known to the world, but it will avail them little unless Germans themselves are ready to betray Germany.'

Adolf Hitler to SS Gen. Schellenberg, 1939

1

EYELESS IN TWELVELAND

As was his habit, the traitor slipped into Cologne's *Hauptbahnhof* by the night train from Holland. Grasping his black briefcase containing his samples and papers which identified him as the Dutch agent for the German automobile firm BMW, he hurried across the square and entered the Hotel Dom, in the shadow of the great Gothic cathedral which dominates the city.

Giskes, from the Hamburg branch of the *Abwehr*,[1] was waiting for him in the lobby. He was in civilian clothes, but there was no mistaking that he was an old-school officer of the Imperial German Army, recently recalled to the service. The two men shook hands; Giskes ordered drinks and they got down to business.

As usual the naturalized Englishman (he had been born Dutch) did most of the talking. But what he said did not seem to interest Giskes and the traitor soon noticed his lack of interest although Giskes let him talk. After all, the Englishman was the only agent who had been assigned to him by his chief, Captain von Feldmann.[2]

Yet it was obvious that the traitor's sources were running dry; it was nearly three years since he had been fired from the Secret Intelligence Service after the suicide of his chief and the resultant scandal. By now, the spring of 1939, most of his contacts with the Continental Secret Intelligence Service were gone. All the same Giskes suspected that he knew

---

[1] The German Secret Service.
[2] Von Feldmann had brought Giskes into the *Abwehr* by urging him not to let himself 'be shot to pieces for that man', i.e. Hitler. As a result Giskes volunteered for the *Abwehr* from his anti-tank unit. In 1940 von Feldmann's prophecy came true: Giskes' former unit was wiped out by the French at the Battle of Sedan.

something important. As he recalled over thirty years later,[3] 'I realized that he had an ace up his sleeve—one vital last card. And I was determined to get it by hook or by crook.'

Giskes finished his drink and put his glass down with an air of finality. 'Let me know when you get some more information,' he said. 'Then we can meet again.'

The traitor looked crestfallen. 'But when can we meet?' he asked.

Giskes shrugged. 'Your stuff is not interesting enough for me to come all the way from Hamburg to meet you.'

There was an awkward silence while Giskes pretended to study his glass, though, as he confessed later, 'I was worried that I'd overdone it. After all he was the only agent I had.'

'I know a man,' the traitor said. 'But if I tell you his name, you'll hang him.' He looked appealingly at Giskes, as if he wanted confirmation that he wouldn't.

'I can't guarantee it, but I'll promise you that I'll do my best to save him,' Giskes assured him.

The traitor considered this for some time and Giskes realized that he had been right; he did have something. He needed money and he knew that his embellishing of old tales would no longer suffice to keep Admiral Canaris[4] paying him.

Giskes tried a new track. 'How much do you want?' The traitor talked around the subject for a while, until Giskes interrupted him. 'Look, I'll give you five thousand guilders if your information is important.'

Still he hesitated. 'I can't tell you his name.' Giskes pulled out his pencil and tossed it on to the table. 'Then write it!'

'His name is Krueger,' the traitor reluctantly replied.

'There are thousands of Kruegers in Germany; I'll want more details than that.' He took out a wad of notes and put them on the table in front of him.

'His full name is Otto Krueger. The British call him Doctor Krueger. He lives in Godesberg near Bonn, but he

[3] In a conversation with the author.
[4] The head of the *Abwehr*.

comes to Holland for his meetings with the station head[5] and stays in the Amstel in Amsterdam or in the Hotel des Indes at The Hague.'

In the elegant comfort of Cologne's best hotel, the traitor betrayed Britain's super-spy, her longest-serving agent in Germany, a man whose code number was still classified in London long after the war.[6]

A few minutes later the two men parted. They were not to see each other again for six years; and when they did it would be Giskes' turn to send the traitor to his death just as he had sent Krueger on that warm spring evening in 1939.

The traitor's name was Hooper, John William (Jack) Hooper, and up to 1936 he had been the trusted assistant of Major Hugh Reginald Dalton, head of the SIS station in Holland.

The main task of the station, located at 57 Nieuwe Parklaan, The Hague, was to spy on the newly resurgent Germany, and Dalton had done a good job building up a network of agents in that country, who filed their reports with Hooper.

On 4 September, 1936, Dalton was found shot dead in his flat. At first foul play was suspected. After all he was a long-time spymaster. Soon, however, SIS investigators from London established that Dalton had committed suicide; he had embezzled SIS funds in order to keep his mistress. They also discovered that Hooper, his loyal assistant, had found out that his chief had been dipping his hand into the till and had been blackmailing him. Naturally enough the SIS investigators could not hand Hooper over to the civilian police. The alternative was to have him murdered. Surprisingly enough the SIS authorities vetoed that way out[7] and Hooper was allowed to go free. Four months later he began to betray the British spy network to the *Abwehr* bit

---

[5] Head of the local Secret Intelligence Service.   [6] It was 33016.

[7] In a conversation with the author, Giskes said that he was surprised the British did not get rid of Hooper in the 'conventional' way. After all in the First World War they often dropped spies and traitors into one of Holland's canals—a very convenient way of getting rid of such trash.

by bit, giving Captain von Feldmann, and later Captain Hermann Giskes, new details and fresh names each time he ran out of money, which was often.

By the spring of 1939, information about the SIS network run from The Hague was at a premium in Germany. Until the previous summer the chief Continental base for British Intelligence had been in Vienna.

Here Captain Thomas Kendrick, working from the traditional cover of His Majesty's Passport Office, had penetrated Germany with a very effective spy-ring. But in the spring of 1938, Kendrick had been arrested when the Germans occupied Austria.

Then the centre of anti-German espionage shifted to Copenhagen. But in November of that year the Danes started a big spy hunt. One of the men they arrested was a German named Waldemar Poetsch, who belonged to the SIS's sabotage organization, which had been blowing up German, Italian and Spanish freighters carrying strategic goods. At first the Danes thought they had arrested a German spy. When they discovered he was working for the British they held his trial *in camera*, in order not to embarrass the British Government, but the *Abwehr* managed to procure the details of his activities. They also bribed the assistant to the Copenhagen Chief-of-Police and obtained further information about the British spy-ring in Denmark from him.[8] Thus the SIS were obliged to leave Copenhagen and The Hague became the centre of the German espionage rings.

Under the command of the newly appointed Major Henry Richard Stevens, of whom we shall hear more later, the Dutch section of the SIS operated in more or less independent groups—political, economic, military and naval.

Its agents came from the vast reservoir of German refugees who had fled to Holland after the National Socialist take-over in Germany in 1933—Jewish, monarchist, socialist,

[8] The *Abwehr* tried to kidnap Poetsch from his Copenhagen jail. The Danes tipped off the SIS and the spy was smuggled out of the country on a freighter. It was then suggested that the *Abwehr* should hijack the freighter to a German Baltic port, but Admiral Canaris vetoed that proposal as not being in accordance with his conception of the *Abwehr* as a club for gentlemen'.

even communist—the whole spectrum of anti-Nazi resistance. There was, for instance, the network of former Catholic youth groups, now banned, centred on Dr Hans Ebeling, a former Dusseldorf journalist, and youth leader Theo Hespers from Moenchen-Gladbach. The latter had fled from Germany in 1933 and settled near Roermond on the German border. He knew the area well from his camping days with the Gladbach youth movement. Using the chain of Catholic monasteries which ran along the border (his aunt was an abbess in a nunnery), he easily managed to keep in contact with his former comrades in Germany. He also used the daily shipments of vegetables from Holland to the Reich to smuggle in anti-Nazi propaganda.

In 1936 the German authorities became aware of his activities, when he used a furniture van to smuggle in several tons of anti-Nazi propaganda, and protested to the Dutch Government. The latter banned him from the province of Limburg, in which Roermond is located, and he was forced to move inland to Helmond in North Brabant.

Penniless and unable to find a job (the Dutch made it hard for the refugees to obtain employment in the hope that they would move on), he was easy meat for Dr Ebeling when the latter approached him with an offer to work for the SIS. Thereafter Theo Hespers travelled widely—Belgium, Switzerland, France, Ireland, England—and in 1937 began to publish an anti-Nazi monthly.

But now his old contacts in Germany were used not just to spread propaganda against the new régime, but also to collect information for Dr Ebeling who was living in London.[9]

There was also a social democrat ring called 'Willem II', named for Gerhard Hubert Willems, a 27-year-old socialist, mechanic and six-day cycle racer. Another SIS group was composed of German aristocrats, such as Count von Spiegel-Siesenberg and Baron von Gerlach, which was managed by a career German Foreign Ministry official Wolfgang von

[9] Theo Hespers suffered a tragic fate. He was not executed in the wake of the 'Venlo' affair, as was believed in London. According to his son he got as far as Dunkirk in 1940 where the British agreed to evacuate him but not his family. Thereafter he went underground until his arrest in 1942. He was hanged in 1943.

Putlitz, who, in spite of his years and diplomatic manner, was violently anti-Nazi.

There was even a ring which had penetrated right to the top of the organization to which Captain Giskes belonged—the *Abwehr*! For Major Stevens had a link with the chief of Dutch Military Intelligence, General van Orschoot (he was carried on the station list of spies as 'Agent No. 945') who supplied him occasionally with information obtained by the Dutch military attaché in Berlin, Colonel Jan Sas.

Sas, a pleasant-mannered, self-effacing officer, had established a working relationship with Colonel Hans Oster, Admiral Canaris' chief-of-staff and grey eminence of the German Secret Service. A convinced opponent of the Nazi régime, he supplied Sas with information when it suited his purpose, in the knowledge it would reach the SIS in due course.[10]

But in the mass of amateur agents, Otto Krueger stood out by virtue of his sheer length of service, his professionalism, and above all his tremendous range of contacts throughout German industrial and military circles. Even thirty years after his death a senior member of the SIS could remember his code number immediately and remark that 'He was absolutely brilliant. The Royal Navy relied upon him almost exclusively for their information about activities of their opposite numbers within Germany.' Now, after Hooper and another traitor[11] in the ranks of the SIS in Holland had betrayed some forty agents to the *Abwehr* in 1938–9, he, too, was to be arrested.

'They were aghast in Hamburg when I told them about Krueger,' Giskes recalls today. 'Some of them even knew him personally!'

Otto Krueger had been an engineering lieutenant commander in the old Imperial Navy during the First World

---

[10] How Colonel Oster managed to remain in his post for so long remains a mystery to this day. His anti-Nazi attitude was well known to the rank-and-file of the *Abwehr* even *before* the war. The then Captain N. Ritter recollects that as early as 1938 he refused to shake hands with his nominal superior because he was 'so obviously a traitor'.

[11] A Dutchman, working for the SIS, named van Koutrik.

War. In the years after the war, he had been recruited into the Secret Intelligence Service to keep an eye on his old comrades of the *Kriegsmarine*.

With the aid of British money and his own native talent, he had prospered during the Weimar Republic and even more so after the National Socialist take-over. One of Germany's celebrated *technische Hochschulen* awarded him an honorary doctorate and in the middle 'thirties he was elected to the directorate of the Federation of German Industries.

For nearly twenty years he had been able to conduct his remarkable double life without anyone suspecting he was a British spy, in spite of the fact that he lived in considerable style. The SIS payments for his services were camouflaged as returns from his inventions patented in the United Kingdom and Holland.

Now, in the spring of 1939, the *Abwehr*, working hand-in-hand with the Reich Main Security Office, went to work on Dr Krueger. The Gestapo checked his mail, his phone, his bank account, his private life—without result. Everything seemed above board. He had no expensive vices; he wasn't addicted to drugs; he was not a homosexual nor did he keep a mistress. Twenty years of leading a double life had obviously taught him to be exceedingly careful.

Then, in July, 1939, after paying a visit to Hamburg's Blohm & Voss shipyard, which did a great deal of work for the *Kriegsmarine*, Dr Otto Krueger left for Holland on another of his business trips. Now it was the turn of the *Abwehr* again.[12]

At their meeting at the Hotel Dom in April, Hooper had told Giskes that it was during his trips to Holland that Krueger really revealed himself as a spy. Accordingly the *Abwehr* planted its agents in both the hotels known to be frequented by Krueger and arranged for him to be shadowed the whole time he was in Holland. But Krueger seemed to do nothing out of the ordinary. He remained most of the first day in his hotel room typing. Then in the evening he

[12] As was the case with the SIS, the *Abwehr* had no power of arrest; that was left to the Gestapo. But in the pre-war period the Gestapo did not operate outside Germany's frontiers.

went out to dine with a business associate and his wife. Later he drove out to a villa in the suburb of Scheveningen, returning to his hotel about midnight.

The watchers were perplexed. Krueger's behaviour was beyond suspicion. Was Hooper lying after all?

Then a retired *Abwehr* spy-catcher, Commander Trautgott Andreas Richard Protze, an old colleague of Admiral Canaris himself, stepped in. He found out that the villa in Scheveningen was owned by a man named August de Fremery. He contacted his own traitor in the SIS, van Koutrik. 'Does the name August de Fremery mean anything to you?'

The Dutch traitor, who had already betrayed von Putlitz to the *Abwehr*,[13] answered immediately. 'Of course. It's the real name of "Jan", our Captain Hendricks.'

Commander Protze knew he had Krueger at last. Captain Hendricks was none other than the deputy head of the SIS station in The Hague!

On 7 July, 1939, Otto Krueger, Agent 33016, was arrested and confessed everything to the Gestapo the same day. Britain's key agent in Nazi Germany was finished; soon the rest of the small fry would follow him behind bars.[14] On the eve of war, the SIS was virtually eyeless in Twelveland. Now it was time for 'Cotton's Circus' to take a hand.

[13] Von Putlitz managed to escape and during the war worked for the British in the 'black' propaganda department run by ex-*Daily Express* reporter Sefton Delmer.

[14] One day after Britain declared war on Germany, Otto Krueger killed himself in Hamburg's *Stadtgefaengnis*.

2

COTTON'S CIRCUS

In the summer of 1938, Frederick Sidney Cotton, an Australian pilot, arrived in London. He was a man who loved adventure, and as one of the women who was to become famous because of his pioneering work was later to remark: 'If (he) had lived a few centuries earlier he would have made a splendid buccaneer, for he had a notable record for getting what he wanted by hook or by crook.'[1]

Another female associate who knew him at that time was more drastic in her assessment. 'Cotton was completely unscrupulous,' she recalls, 'and a tremendous skirt-chaser. He ran a whole string of mistresses and when he was finished with them he would invariably marry them off to some unsuspecting fool or other.'[2]

To the chiefs of the British SIS, looking for a man to undertake a completely new form of intelligence, it must have seemed that Frederick Sidney Cotton was just the man they wanted, more especially as his new London-based colour photography firm was going to take him to Germany a lot.

Thus it was, after the SIS had sounded Cotton out in Paris, that he received a telephone call in London.

'Major Cotton? I understand that you have just returned from Paris where you met my friend Paul?'

'Yes, that is so.' Cotton felt the other man's voice was 'superbly anonymous', but he asked for no further details of the caller's business.

'I'd like to come and see you right away if I may.'

Cotton agreed and a few minutes later a 'Major' Winter-

[1] Constance Smith, *Evidence in Camera.*
[2] In conversation with the author.

botham appeared.[3] Cotton shook hands with the 'Major' and they sat down to talk. Half an hour later he was a surprised, if somewhat more prosperous, temporary member of His Majesty's Secret Intelligence Service.

Frederick Winterbotham, the career SIS officer who had recruited Cotton and dreamed up this new departure, which was to be the start of scientific intelligence as we know it today, was a handsome ex-World War One RFC pilot, who had joined the SIS in 1929 after an unsuccessful post-war career as a sheep farmer.

When it became clear that Twelveland was British Intelligence's primary target he was sent to that country periodically under the guise of being anticommunist—which he was—and pro-Nazi—which he wasn't—to check the progress of Germany's rearmament in the air.

Between 1932 and 1938 he met most of Germany's leaders, including Hitler. However it was Rosenberg, a minister and the National Socialists' chief ideologist, who took a special liking to him and wrote of him in his diary: 'A most important officer . . . a firm believer that Germans and English should stand together in the defence against the Bolshevik danger.'

In 1937 at a party in the course of which Rosenberg became 'really sloshed', the Nazi leader warned Winterbotham that his true role as a spy had become known to the German authorities through the agency of their Italian allies who had shadowed him everywhere he had gone the previous year in Italy. Winterbotham took the warning to heart but his superiors were desperate for high-level intelligence about the German leaders' thinking at this time and so he went back to the Third Reich one year later to spend a holiday with Erich Koch, the *Gauleiter* of East Prussia. However, he found that 'good and reliable information coming out of Germany was being seriously curtailed'. Thus he decided that a new means must be found to obtain the vital details of what was going on in Twelveland. But how?

[3] His rank was just as fake as Cotton's but it was assumed for different reasons.

14

In 1917 young Captain Winterbotham had been shot down in northern France while flying as a fighter escort to a slow-moving photographic reconnaissance plane. He had escaped with his life, but during his imprisonment in Germany, which had ended in Trier at an old school where Karl Marx himself had once studied, he had reflected at length on the methods used by the RFC. To him they seemed to be 'unnecessarily risky and totally unimaginative—always the same procedure: the rendezvous of the Scouts and Photographic Flight near enough to give the enemy plenty of warning, the long dive down to get within proper height of the target, the massed anti-aircraft fire, the swarms of enemy fighters, the dog-fights and the losses'.

Over twenty years later, with the SIS sources of intelligence in Germany drying up one after another, Winterbotham began to toy with the idea of using planes to gather intelligence. Why not use the wartime method of air reconnaissance to keep track of German preparations for the coming conflict?

Winterbotham knew that his French opposite number in the *Deuxième Bureau*, Georges Ronin, had already bribed personnel of Air France to take hurried snapshots of German military installations while their planes flew over Twelveland; and from the French side of the Rhine, he had flown a very old plane up and down the river while a bearded Parisian portrait photographer had operated an ancient wooden camera photographing the German fortifications on the other side.

He put forward his idea to the Chief of the Air Staff, Sir Cyril Newall, and it was approved. He was given the money to buy an American Lockheed 12A, a twin-engined executive aircraft, which could fly up to 22,000 feet, higher than any known German fighter at that time. Georges Ronin, in Paris, persuaded his government to do the same.

The next problem was to find 'the right type of aerial James Bond', as Winterbotham recalled. He found him in the person of Sidney Cotton. Winterbotham took an instant dislike to the Australian. He was 'too big for his boots' and above all 'greedy'. All the same he hired him and early in 1939 set him up in a small company named Aeronautical

Research and Sales with his offices near the SIS HQ in St James's Square. Cotton was given an allowance of two hundred pounds a month, a flat for himself and his current mistress, and an assistant, a young Canadian pilot named Bob Niven who had just finished a short-service commission with the RAF.

Now it was up to the 'Cotton Circus' to solve the major technical problem facing this new form of aerial intelligence —a problem which had caused Winterbotham to be shot down in 1917—how to keep out of range of enemy fighters and still take photographs. For in spite of the technical advances made in cameras since 1917, their lenses still fogged with condensation from cold air at over eight thousand feet.

Cotton first of all set about installing the Leica cameras. A hole was cut in the Lockheed's frame and the three cameras installed, one pointing straight downwards and the other two at angles so that the plane could get the maximum coverage of the object being photographed. A concealing shutter was then fixed above the hole so that it looked like the outer skin of the plane. Now came the surprise. On the plane's first trial in England it was discovered that when this concealing shutter was opened from the controls in the heated cabin, warm air was automatically drawn out of the hole over the lenses. As Winterbotham wrote many years later, 'Wonder of wonders they (the lenses) did not fog up, even at a height of twenty thousand feet. It seemed almost too simple to be true!'

By April, 1939, Cotton's Circus was ready to go into action.

Cotton's first flight was a high altitude one along the west German coast on behalf of Naval Intelligence, with his current mistress handling the cameras. It was a complete success save for the fact that the Leicas did not take sufficiently large shots. All the same, as Winterbotham recalls, 'the prints showed us that there was so much going on'.

New RAF cameras were installed and after a major survey

of the Italian activities in the Mediterranean, Cotton started to make his first dummy runs into the heart of Twelveland itself. However, on these first trips the camera was not used. Winterbotham reasoned that they should first check whether the now suspicious Germans might search the Lockheed for cameras. They didn't. Nor did they object to his high altitude flights over important military regions. 'It seemed obvious,' Winterbotham wrote, 'that the Germans had not tumbled to this idea because they raised no objections to a civil aircraft flying anywhere as long as it was flying high enough. It was clear that they had not realized that the British had solved the secret of how to prevent a camera's lenses from clouding over at high altitude.'

Cotton could begin his work in earnest.

On a hot day in July, 1939, the first day of the great Frankfurt Air Rally, Cotton's elegant blue Lockheed—the colour made it virtually invisible from below at great height —landed at the city's large new airport, Frankfurt Main. Taxiing up to join the rest of the arrivals, Cotton allowed the party he had brought with him to disembark. As they included such important figures for German trade as the editor of the *Aeroplane* and Margaret Gilruth, an Australian journalist who was going to write about the show, Cotton's Berlin agent Herr Schoene, a former member of the famous First World War Richthofen Squadron, was able to introduce them to some very important members of the *Luftwaffe* hierarchy. General Milch and General Kesselring both expressed interest in the Lockheed, the first of its type they had seen. In fact Kesselring expressed a desire to fly in the luxuriously appointed American machine.

Cotton said he'd be delighted to take the General for a flight. In fact, he'd let him handle the controls himself if he wished. Kesselring, who had been transferred from the artillery to the *Luftwaffe* after the Nazi take-over and had learned to fly at a late age, was overjoyed at this unexpected opportunity to display his newly acquired skills.

With feigned innocence the Australian suggested that the plane should fly along the Rhine in the direction of

Mannheim. So they set off in the *kolossaler Lockheed* as the excited *Luftwaffe* officers kept calling it. As soon as they were over the Rhine, Cotton handed over the controls to Kesselring, and sat back in the co-pilot's seat. But although his face was outwardly calm, his mind was racing. He knew that Winterbotham dearly wanted to know what progress the Germans had made with the newly built *Luftwaffe* fields in the area. In the end he could not resist the temptation; he knew he'd never get another chance to fly over the prohibited area at this height. He flicked on the cameras which were operated from the dashboard.

After a while the General noticed the green light which was flashing on and off to indicate the continuity of the cameras' exposures. 'What is that light for?' he asked Cotton.

'It's a special device, General, to show the petrol flow to the engines.'

Kesselring was satisfied and the flight continued. The same thing happened the following day, with high-ranking German Air Force officers competing for a flight. As Constance Babington-Smith, to whom Cotton told his adventures in the first year of the war, commented: 'Accompanied by a series of *Luftwaffe* generals and colonels, Cotton flew hither and thither at a couple of thousand feet, over the airfields and ammunition dumps, the factories and fortifications. And while his passengers commented with interest on the Lockheed's performance, Sidney casually flicked a little switch, and down below the cameras went clicking away.'

The pictures Cotton obtained were excellent, and they continued to be excellent in the weeks that followed. Soon the results of Cotton's reconnaissance missions began turning up in all the new top-secret intelligence sections being formed in London, delivered in large buff envelopes accompanied by a slip bearing the legend 'With the Managing Director's compliments'. Competition started to obtain the services of this bold Australian who was producing such tremendous work. A recent recruit to Naval Intelligence, whom one old SIS hand remembers as 'a real snake', even went as far as to offer Cotton a captaincy in the Royal Naval Reserve if he would transfer his services from the SIS to the

DNI. The name of the brash young naval officer was Ian Fleming.

Cotton refused, but as Winterbotham recalled: 'He was getting far too big for his boots. One could almost see the change in him daily. And he wanted more money too.' But as July passed into August and the danger of war loomed ever larger, he continued to work for the SIS, flying even more missions over Twelveland.

On 14 August he had just landed at Berlin's Tempelhof field after taking a more northerly course than usual when the airport's control officer asked to see him. 'Are you not flying from London on rather a roundabout course?' he asked Cotton.

Cotton used a bluff, answering that he always flew on a great circle route.

The German Controller tried to conceal his apparent ignorance by saying: 'Oh, like Lindbergh, eh? Thank you. I beg your pardon for having to ask you.'

When Cotton reported the incident to Winterbotham, the latter realized that the days of Cotton's Circus were numbered. Yet everywhere the powers-that-be were crying out for accurate details of Twelveland's preparations for war—details that only Cotton could obtain. Besides Cotton had grandiose plans of his own.

On the 19th, Cotton was introduced to Colonel Stewart Menzies, acting head of the SIS, and told him that he felt that Goering had more influence on Hitler than anyone else. If he, Cotton, could bring Goering to England and convince him of Britain's will to fight, then the head of the *Luftwaffe* might persuade Hitler to halt his plans to invade Poland.[4]

Menzies, who saw in the impossible mission a real chance to make a name for himself, told Cotton: 'Well done, this might change everything.'

In Cotton's presence he called the Prime Minister, Mr Chamberlain, and within minutes Lord Halifax, the Foreign Minister, said: 'The Prime Minister has agreed to your

---

[4] The means of impressing Goering were to include 'an informal dinner with attractive ladies and good company ... with perhaps some shooting and other relaxations over the next day or so'.

proposal and you will receive a letter . . . saying your friend will be welcome.'

Fred Winterbotham did not like Cotton's 'hare-brained, crackpot scheme one bit'. He told the Australian: 'I don't want you to get caught in Berlin when the balloon goes up. If the situation looks really desperate, I'll cable you saying "Mother is ill". I'll sign it "Mary". When you get that cable come back at once. Otherwise at the very least you'll be interned. If they find out what you've been doing you'll be shot.'

So Cotton flew off with Bob Niven, the Canadian assistant pilot, on his crazy scheme, taking two loose cameras with him in the Lockheed's cabin. As Winterbotham had predicted, the mission was a failure and when Cotton asked for permission to fly back to London he was refused. All civilian flying had been grounded. Hitler had ordered that Poland should be invaded on 26 August.[5] Cotton and Niven were trapped.

On the 24th, however, Hitler postponed the date of the attack and Cotton was given permission to fly back to London on a prescribed flight route and at a height of exactly 300 metres. The German flak batteries had been warned of their flight and if they deviated one metre from course the Lockheed would be shot down immediately.

At 11.15 they were airborne. It was some time before Niven spoke. 'That was a close one,' he said at length.

'Too close,' Cotton replied.

'It's still two hundred and fifty miles to the border,' Niven reminded him. But by sticking rigidly to their course and the prescribed height they managed to avoid trouble. As they crossed the Dutch border, heading for Groningen, the two pilots looked over their right shoulders in the direction of Wilhelmshaven. By some astonishing freak of light, they were able to see the Schilling roads outside the naval port. And glinting in the sun were the ships of the German fleet

[5] Some of the *Abwehr*'s secret units which had been ordered to capture special objectives on the Polish frontier on the 26th actually carried out their missions and had to be hurriedly recalled. Thus the first shots of the new war were fired ironically enough by the *Abwehr*, whose head, Canaris, was conspiring with the British and French to prevent the war!

within their midst the white glimmer of Hitler's own yacht *Die Grille*.

Excitedly they brought out their two hidden Leicas to film them. As Cotton said, 'Here was something that would certainly interest the Admiralty.' Two hours later they landed at Heston to be asked by a customs official: 'Where from?'

'Berlin,' Cotton answered.

'Left it a bit late, haven't you?'

Thus the great air spy game, the forerunner of the ill-fated U-2 and the satellite spies which at this very moment circle the earth some hundred miles above our heads photographing every secret, was over.[6]

Eight days after Cotton's escape from Tempelhof, Winterbotham was duty officer at the Broadway headquarters of the Secret Intelligence Service. In the early hours of the morning of Friday, 1 September, he was roused by an urgent call from the SIS station in Warsaw. The station commander there gave him one single word—the code word for 'war'.

Immediately he picked up the green phone near his camp bed. 'Vicky,' he called to the girl on the switchboard, 'get me the Cabinet Offices on the scrambler, please.'

Seconds later his call was through.

'That you, Cox?' he asked. 'May we scramble? This is Zero C speaking. Just to let you know that the first bombs fell on Warsaw a few minutes ago,' he said calmly, having expected the outbreak of war for months.

'*War! My God!*', Cox gasped at the other end. 'Have you anything else?'

'No. But don't stay up too late. I'm going back to sleep.'

'Zero C' put down the green phone and stretched out on the office camp bed again. He felt quite relaxed. 'The

---

[6] Cotton did, however, fly one more mission with Niven and his current girlfriend operating the cameras. He managed to get back with twenty-four hours to spare. A few weeks later Cotton was absorbed into the RAF's photo reconnaissance section, where he ran Spitfires into Belgium to spy on Britain's future allies. Thereafter he had a conventional war. Afterwards he bought a Lancaster bomber and smuggled an Indian Prince's diamonds out of post-partition India.

ghastly inevitability of this moment had grown step by step over the last six years,' he recalled years later, 'and now World War Two had begun.'

Winterbotham, the sole representative of the Secret Intelligence Service's senior staff on duty that night, closed his eyes. There was nothing more he could do now. In a matter of minutes he was asleep again.

The 'old firm's' battle for Twelveland had started in earnest.[7]

[7] The 'old firm' was the SIS's familiar name for the organization.

3

THE OLD FIRM

In September, 1939, 'C' was dying of cancer. Admiral Hugh Sinclair, the head of the Secret Intelligence Service, 'C' as he was known to the outside world, had only a matter of weeks to live at the very moment when his country needed him most.

The long-time head of the SIS—he had taken over the post in 1923—was wasting away daily. His stocky figure had shrunk and his smile—'like the welcoming smile of a benign uncle'—was gone.

With two admirals and an air marshal queueing to take over the key post, C's long-time deputy, Colonel Stewart Menzies,[1] who was in charge of military intelligence, managed to convince the dying man that he should sign a letter stating that he, Menzies, should be given the job, at least till the authorities thought otherwise. Thus, on the day the Second World War broke out, Colonel Stewart Menzies, formerly of the Grenadier Guards and the Life Guards, a holder of the DSO and the MC, was the most important member of the SIS.

Aged forty-nine, he was a typical product of his class, interested in sport, clubs and social prestige, with very little time for what he called 'intellectuals' in a manner which indicated that the latter occupied a special place in his personal demonology. He had been educated at Eton, where, according to one contemporary,[2] 'Stewart was a beautiful athlete, winning the steeplechase, probably the most coveted race to win at Eton. As a football player, he captained the XI. He was also Master of the Beagles and the President of

[1] Pronounced 'Meng-is'.
[2] Sir Rex Benson. *The Times*, 6 June, 1968.

"Pop". He had a friendly happy disposition, not easily ruffled.'

From Eton he went to Sandhurst, was commissioned into the Grenadier Guards and then transferred to the Life Guards. After winning an MC in the early battles in France in the First World War, he transferred to the intelligence section of Haig's staff where he served for the rest of the war; and he was to remain in intelligence for the rest of his career, slowly working his way up to become Sinclair's deputy.

According to one story King George VI once pressed him to reveal details of his service. Jokingly the Monarch said, 'Menzies, what would happen if I were to ask you the name of our man in Berlin?'

The Colonel replied, 'I should have to say, Sir, that my lips are sealed.'

'Well, supposing I were to say, "Off with your head"?'

'In that case, Sir, my head would roll with the lips still sealed!'

In 1939 when he moved into C's office on the fourth floor of Broadway Buildings, he was a pale, reticent man who tried to keep a distance between himself and his staff. In order to know what was going on in the SIS's various departments, he employed two special wartime assistants; one, Boyle, was known to the old SIS hands as 'creeping Jesus' and generally regarded as the 'chief's spy'. The other, Koch de Gooreynd, had been a minor hero of the gossip columns, his sole claim to fame being that he had been one of the first in the country to own a home cinematograph.

As one of the wartime 'intellectual' recruits to the SIS, the future Regius Professor of Modern History at Oxford, Hugh Trevor-Roper, commented on Menzies: 'He was a bad judge of men and drew his personal advisers from a painfully limited social circle which was quite incapable of giving him the support he needed. I do not think that he ever really understood the war in which he was engaged.'

But in 1939 Menzies was more concerned with holding on to his new post. One long-time SIS executive remembers him at that time: 'He ruled from a large office behind a padded door guarded by his secretary Miss Pettigrew. There he sat behind a vast antique desk, which it was reputed that M. W. Cummings, head of SIS in the First World War, had pinched and had once belonged to Nelson. When the green light outside his office went on, you could go in and there he would twiddle his pen back and forth—the use of green ink for signing correspondence written on pale blue paper was reserved for him—while he listened to you. When you touched on anything which interested him, he automatically stopped playing with his pen. After a while you came to realize that when he began to twiddle with the pen again, he had made a decision. But he rarely revealed what that decision was—even to the senior men in the Service.'

For, in spite of his ability to conceal his emotions, Colonel Menzies was desperately insecure that September, fighting in the shadows to retain his new position. 'He was very good at interdepartmental manoeuvring,' one wartime SIS officer recalls. Another, who had worked with Menzies for over a decade, was more drastic in his estimate of the new chief's character: '[He was] totally disloyal to anyone but himself ... When "Quex" Sinclair died, he virtually sacrificed all the really good men in SIS to hold on to his slippery chair and placate the influential job-seekers. The list of his dirty tricks is a long one. Result, he was so hard up for loyal assistants that he brought back the most unpopular snake in the business who had been banished from the UK by Quex for some unspeakable reason, and took on Claude Dansey as his No. 2. It led to nothing but discord.'

Claude Dansey had been a territorial officer in the First World War, seconded to Intelligence. He had resigned his commission in the 'twenties to try his luck in the United States, where he opened a country club in which rich Americans were served in the style of the English landed gentry. The venture failed and he returned to the SIS, where his ability to 'scatter his venom at long range'[3] forced Admiral Sinclair to ban him from the office.

He asked Sinclair if he could go abroad to build up a new SIS outfit on the Continent. Without the Admiral's blessing but with funds supplied by the department, Dansey

[3] Kim Philby's description of him.

went first to Rome and then to Switzerland where he established the melodramatically named 'Z' organization.

Now this man who was outspokenly anti-intellectual—'I would never willingly employ a university graduate', he was once reported to have said—returned to London to become, in effect, Menzies' second-in-command. His return was a tremendous shock for the third member of the strange triumvirate which was to govern Britain's Intelligence Service during the war, Colonel Valentine 'Vee-Vee' Vivian.

Vivian, the son of a Victorian portrait painter, was a complete contrast to Dansey, both physically and mentally. Whereas Dansey was rough and tough, Vivian was lean and elegant. He had come from the British Indian Police into the SIS and was in fact Sinclair's oldest assistant, senior to Menzies himself. But he had allowed himself to be elbowed out by Menzies; and he was no match for Dansey, who despised him.

As a pre-war SIS man remembers him, 'Poor old Vivian. He was totally without imagination, a waffler . . . a charming, harmless, meticulous, conscientious policeman . . . [who] had a brilliant assistant, Felix Cowgill, who did the real wartime job.'

Now the two men squared up to each other. When it was suggested that each section within the SIS should have a separate colour-code, Dansey wrote in the margin of the memo: 'I suggest yellow would be a suitable colour for this section'. The section in question was Vivian's.

On another occasion he described Vivian's staff as 'a lot of old women in red flannel knickers!'

In retaliation Vivian buried himself in his own section—counter-intelligence—jealously guarding its independence from Dansey's section concerned with supervising the intelligence-gathering networks. Soon the two chief assistants were not talking to each other unless forced to by their chief. Dansey hogged Menzies' office after working hours so that Vivian was unable to get in to see his boss. Vivian, in his turn, always went on leave when Menzies did so that he would not be forced to take orders from Dansey; and he deliberately started recruiting university graduates into the SIS.

26

Strange men indeed to run the organization which was to be Britain's 'eyes and ears' on the Continent for the next five years!

Their subordinates were no less strange. In the main the permanent SIS officers came from two classes: 'metropolitan young gents' recruited in clubs such as White's or Boodle's by Colonel Dansey; or ex-Indian Policemen selected from the New Delhi Central Intelligence Bureau by Colonel Vivian. During the course of the *Sunday Times* inquiry into the 'Philby affair', David Leitch, one of the reporters involved, asked an old SIS hand about the early wartime recruitment practices of the organization. Leitch said: 'They seem to have got most of these chaps out of the bar at White's so far as one can see.'

The ex-SIS man replied: 'Yes, well you wouldn't find anything except crooks there, would you?'

'And where were you recruited?'

'Boodle's.'[4]

In the main, the rank-and-file of the SIS were heavy on brawn and light in brains: rugby blues whose weakness for skirt-chasing abroad attracted unwelcome attention from the police; 'thinkers' whose only answer to international communism was a device to smuggle moths into Russian cinemas which when released would cast black shadows across the screen; senior officers who spent long lunches at the Savoy discussing how to weaken Japanese resistance by infecting the sanitary towels of their womenfolk with some unmentionable disease.

They were bold, daring young men, who felt they were doing an important job for their country against the background of an often hostile and dangerous environment, with imprisonment or possibly death as the price of failure; but they were fitted neither by education or training for the complexities of the new war against Twelveland, with its intelligence services filled with what Shirer has called 'intellectual gangsters'.

[4] Quoted in *Philby: The Spy Who Betrayed a Generation* by Page, Leitch and Knightley.

And even if the new recruits to the SIS were themselves intellectually superior to the pre-war types—Colonel Vivian was very proud of the influx of writers, journalists and ex-university teachers, 'my intellectuals', as he called them—they, too, were often dubious.

There was, for instance, the hard-drinking, homosexual Guy Burgess whose contacts were to be found in the international 'gay' network, such as von Putlitz and Edouard Pfeiffer, the Chief-of-Cabinet to the French Premier, Daladier.

Burgess once told a friend how he had first met his important French contact playing ping-pong with another homosexual, both immaculately attired in tailcoats and striped pants—*and using as a net a young, completely naked, professional bicycle racer!*

There was the sharp-tongued journalist Malcolm Muggeridge, who in post-war years has never missed an opportunity of satirizing and maligning the service to which he belonged for five years. Three decades after his recruitment to the SIS, he described part of his 'training course' as follows: 'My tour of instruction ended with a short course in invisible inks and their uses. This took place in a house in Hans Crescent, so innocent looking outside, with its trim curtains and array of milk bottles by the front door, that I thought I must have mistaken the address.'

Muggeridge hadn't. His instructor, a 'sad-looking man with a large rubicund face', was waiting for him and quickly instructed him in the means of invisible writing. According to the sad-looking SIS agent, when everything else failed, something he 'referred to primarily as BS, meaning bird shit' could be used.

'But procuring a supply was not as easy as might be supposed. For instance, he once had to fall back on it when he was stationed at The Hague and had imagined that crumbs spread out on his little balcony would bring a goodly number of sparrows along that might be relied on to leave behind a supply of BS.'

He was mistaken. The birds had eaten up the crumbs but had left no droppings behind them. In the end the doleful instructor had been forced to go into a public park where he had dropped his handkerchief as if by chance every time he 'saw traces of BS' and scooped them up. As Muggeridge commented thirty years later: 'What were we at? What was it all about? How had we been induced, two grown men not totally incapable of making some contribution, however lowly, to human existence—how had we been induced to spend our time thus?'

In the end he passed through the door at the house in Hans Crescent, shouting at his instructor in parting: 'I'll remember BS!'

And there was the stuttering ex-*Times* war correspondent, Harold Adrian Russell Philby, known as 'Kim'.

After being quizzed in the forecourt of the St Ermin's Hotel near St James's Park Station by Miss Marjorie Maxse, 'an intensely likeable elderly lady', Philby was invited to meet Vivian for a 'vetting'. The vetting took the form of a luncheon with Vivian, to which Philby's father St John Philby, who had just been released from jail as a suspected Nazi sympathizer, was invited.

When Kim went out to the lavatory, Vivian asked his father, whom he had known in India before the First World War, 'He was a bit of a communist, wasn't he?'

'Oh, that was all schoolboy nonsense,' St John answered. 'He's a reformed character now.'

Vivian was satisfied. After all, as he recalled later, 'I knew his people'.

Thus the arch-traitor and long-time communist agent passed into the service of Britain's most secret organization to become the head of the section which would be concerned with spying on Russia after the Second World War.

Thus Britain's long-established intelligence service prepared to enter the fight against the Germans, who in less than eight years had established one of the most ruthless and efficiently organized counter-espionage services the world has ever seen. As Hugh Trevor-Roper commented: 'When I looked coolly at the world in which I found myself I sometimes thought that if this was our intelligence system we were doomed to defeat.'

4

INCIDENT AT VENLO

Just before midnight on 8 November, 1939, the direct-line telephone to Berlin started to ring at the bedside of Gruppen-führer Schellenberg of the *Sicherheitsdienst*. Schellenberg groped for the phone and grunted 'Hallo'.

At the other end an excited voice snapped, 'What did you say?'

'Nothing so far,' said Schellenberg, who headed the SS's own secret service. 'Who am I speaking to?'

'This is the Reichsführer SS, Heinrich Himmler,' the voice at the other end said sharply. 'Are you there at last?'

Schellenberg woke up at once. 'Yes, sir.'

'Well, listen carefully. Do you know what has happened?'

Schellenberg said that he did not.

'This evening just after the Führer's speech in the Beer Cellar an attempt was made to assassinate him! A bomb went off.[1] Luckily he'd left the cellar a few minutes before. Several old Party comrades have been killed and the damage is pretty considerable. There's no doubt that the British Secret Service is behind it all. The Führer and I were already on his train to Berlin when we got the news. He says, *and this is an order*, when you meet the British agents for your conference tomorrow you are to arrest them immediately and bring them to Germany. This may mean a violation of the Dutch frontier but the Führer says that's of no consequence. The SS detachment that's been assigned to protect you—which, by the way, you certainly don't

[1] Every year on 8 November, which was the anniversary of the 1923 Munich *Putsch*, Hitler gave a speech to old comrades in the beer cellar where the *Putsch* had been planned. In 1939 a somewhat unbalanced workman named Georg Fiser planted a time-bomb in a pillar just behind the spot where Hitler habitually spoke.

deserve after the way you've been behaving—this detachment is to help you to carry out your mission. Do you understand everything?'

Schellenberg knew that the order meant the end of his plan to penetrate the SIS even further. He knew, too, that it would be senseless to argue the point with Himmler; once the *Reichsführer* had made up his mind, he prided himself on the fact that he never changed it.

He said, 'Yes sir,' and rang off.

When Colonel Dansey, the creator of the 'Z' organization, was recalled to England he had ordered his senior commander, Captain Payne Best, to move his group in with Major Stevens' SIS organization located in the passport office at The Hague.

It had been a fatal move; although Hooper had now returned to the fold and was working for the SIS again, the second traitor, von Koutrik, was still supplying the *Abwehr* with information. In a matter of three weeks, he had betrayed the whole network to the Germans and its members in Germany were quietly rounded up by the Gestapo.[2]

It was at this time, when their whole network had been compromised, that Best and Stevens decided to penetrate the highest circles of the Reich. Their decision was based on a visit by two courageous anti-Nazi Germans to London just before the war. The two men, Ewald von Kleist-Schmenzin and Ferdinand von Schlabrendorff, had tried to enlist the support of the British Government in a plot to assassinate Hitler and overthrow the National Socialist régime, which had been engineered by a group of Army officers, clergymen, government officials and social-democrats.[3]

---

[2] According to Giskes the *Abwehr* already had a lead on Best. Prior to the outbreak of war, the economic branch of Hamburg counter-intelligence sent Giskes a photo for identification, which showed a group of visitors at the works' outing of a big German firm. One of the group was an 'Englishman who always seemed to be turning up at these affairs'. The Englishman, Giskes realized later, was Best doing a bit of industrial espionage.

[3] Ironically enough Lt Albrecht Herzner, who had volunteered to

31

Their mission was a failure in two senses. Not only did the British Government turn them down but a spy in the British Foreign Office revealed the details of their plot to a man of very different character to Admiral Canaris, half implicated as he was himself in the plot to get rid of Hitler, a man animated by such utter ruthlessness that Hitler himself described him as 'the man with the iron heart'. His name was Reinhard Tristan Eugen Heydrich.[4]

In October, 1939, when Heydrich took a hand in the plot to infiltrate the SIS, he had just been created head of the Reich's Main Security Office, which grouped every police or intelligence activity (save the *Abwehr*), from customs to the Gestapo, under his control. At the age of thirty-five he was, in essence, the most powerful man behind the scenes in the whole of Nazi Germany.

Tall, blond and always immaculately uniformed, his long, highly intelligent face was marred only by his restless, strangely angled eyes which darted back and forth, never seeming to rest. His figure was that of a highly trained athlete—he was a champion fencer. But it was marred by fat hips.[5]

Yet this man with so much power at his command had an outsize chip on his shoulder, which dated back to his youth when he had been tormented by his schoolmates on account of his high-pitched falsetto voice, his girlish hips, his violin-playing (his father was a music teacher; his mother an actress) and their suspicion that he was Jewish.

Almost instinctively he set out to challenge his schoolmates in toughness. When he walked back and forth to school, he did so with one foot in the gutter and the other on the pavement, never swerving from his course, fighting anyone who got in his way. Once he climbed on the school

help to assassinate Hitler, was in charge of the *Abwehr*'s special squad. which took the Polish Jablunkov Pass on 26 August, 1939, *six full days, four hours and forty-five minutes before the war broke out.*

[4] Historians have often puzzled about the identity of the spy in the Foreign Office. According to Giskes it was a secretary in the Foreign Office of the Under-Secretary, Sir Robert Vansittart.

[5] In spite of being a great womanizer—'black, brown, white or yellow, it didn't matter to him', as one former colleague remembers—he would still dress up as a woman during the course of a long drinking bout.

roof and one hundred feet above the ground balanced his way along a narrow ledge with the horrified teachers and pupils staring up at him as he took his life into his hands.

His adult career in the peacetime German navy had been little different—he had served for a while in Admiral Canaris' ship as a cadet-officer—until he had come a cropper on account of an unsavoury affair with a woman, which had resulted in his being cashiered.

Thus at the height of the German depression in 1931, he had been left jobless, with no other training to fit him for civilian life save that of a naval signals officer. But his new wife, a tall nordic beauty, who was a member of the National Socialist Party, put him in contact with Heinrich Himmler, the leader of the SS. So it was that on 14 June, 1931, he met the bespectacled ex-chicken farmer for the first time and was given twenty minutes to draw up a plan for the formation of a future SS counter-espionage service.[6]

Drawing on his memories of the cheap novels he had read about the British Secret Service, he submitted a plan which Himmler accepted and which was to become the design for the greatest counter-espionage network the world has ever seen.

'The born intelligence officer', as Himmler called him, had a boundless appetite for secret information. '[He was] a living card index, a brain which held all the threads and wove them together,' Kersten, Himmler's intimate, said of him; and this 'living card index' soon spun a web of 100,000 informers all over Germany. He developed a system of lists and cards which kept track of every conceivable opponent of the National Socialist régime, German or foreign. Within a year of the Nazis taking over, an iron curtain, controlled by Heydrich, descended on Germany's frontiers and no one could leave or enter without the permission of the master of Number 8, Prinz Albrecht Strasse, Berlin.[7]

Heydrich was still young and was given to the foibles of young men, which sometimes seem a little ludicrous. Somehow or other he had discovered that the head of the

[6] I am indebted to Frau Linda Heydrich for most of these details about her husband.
[7] The HQ of the Reich's Main Security Office.

British Secret Intelligence Service was referred to as 'C'.[8] Soon after, Heydrich began to imitate this. A rubber stamp was made with the words 'submit to C'. The single initial started to appear in official documents as, 'C has ordered' and 'the decision concerns C personally'. Just like his opposite number, Heydrich reserved the right to be the sole user of green ink for his signature and he had a green light fitted outside his office to signal when visitors might enter, just as C did.

But in spite of his youth, his almost pathological desire to be number one and the James Bond world in which he and his young 'intellectual gangsters' lived, Heydrich was a very formidable opponent, even for a century-old service of which his own experts would soon write: '[Intelligence is] a field in which the British, by virtue of their tradition, their experience, and certain facets of their national character— unscrupulousness, self-control, cool deliberateness and ruthless action—have achieved an unquestionable degree of mastery.'[9]

It was to Heydrich that Schellenberg reported in October, 1939. Heydrich explained to him, 'For several months now we have maintained a very interesting contact directly with British Intelligence. By placing misleading material in their hands, we have succeeded in penetrating their organization. The point has now arrived when we must decide whether we want to continue this game or break it off and be satisfied with what we have learned. I feel you are the right man to take over this affair and I want you to get all the material on it immediately and study it carefully; form your opinions and then give me your recommendations.'

Schellenberg had discovered that a double-agent, F479, who had been a genuine political refugee from the Third Reich before he had returned to the fold to work for Heydrich, had managed to link up with Best as the supposed contact man with the German opposition to Hitler. Best had

---

[8] Group-Captain Winterbotham informs me that it was a punishable offence to reveal this initial prior to the outbreak of the war.

[9] *Informationsheft GB*: an analysis of certain British institutions, printed in Berlin in August 1940, for distribution to the German forces which were to invade England.

swallowed the bait and was firmly convinced that the refugee was genuine.

Schellenberg had not hesitated very long. Almost immediately he had made contact with Best, assuming the guise of monocle-wearing *Hauptmann* Schaemmel of the German General Staff's Transport Service. On 21 October he met Best for the first time. Everything went off smoothly. Eight days later he met him again. This time, however, Best used his connections with Dutch Intelligence to have Schellenberg and his companion arrested at the Dutch frontier and their baggage inspected. While the Dutch police were doing so, Schellenberg saw in his kit a pack of aspirins labelled '*SS Sanitaetshauptamt*' (Main SS Medical Office). Hastily he grabbed the pack and jammed it, paper and all, down his throat and managed to swallow it without the Dutch noticing. Finally the Dutch released them and thereafter Best and Stevens had no further doubts about 'Schaemmel' and his companion.

Now the sudden news of the attempt on Hitler's life changed everything. The time for talk was over. Now 'the man with the iron heart' wanted action.

The November morning was damp and dull. The weather depressed Captain Payne Best. He didn't like the location that the German 'resisters' had chosen for the day's meeting, the red-brick Café Backus near the Dutch frontier town of Venlo with its big plate windows looking out on to a wall of dense undergrowth. As he recalled after the war: 'It would be so easy for some SS men to cross the border at the back of the café and creep up so that they could shoot us through the windows as we sat in the light.'[10] Best was also worried that an 'unpleasant-looking stout man' had given them very searching looks the last time they had been to the café to meet the Germans. But he dismissed his forebodings and went to pick up Stevens at ten o'clock. Stevens also felt that

[10] The café is still there, exactly as it was at the time of the 'incident'. For those who are interested in hearing the story from the horse's mouth, the owner of the little grocery store next to the café is the original owner of the Café Backus.

'the Huns were becoming an infernal nuisance with their shilly-shallying. If the General (the high-ranking 'resister' they hoped to meet) did not come up to scratch this time, we would wash our hands of the whole business and leave them to run their show alone. We would keep this one last appointment and then, finis.'

Stevens handed Best a Browning automatic and pocketed one himself 'just in case'. Lieutenant Klop, a member of Dutch Intelligence, appeared and together they went to collect Best's car which was kept at the Binckhorststraat Garage owned by a Dutchman named Jan Lemmens, who was to drive them to the frontier.[11]

Thus the four men, the two English agents and the two Dutchmen, set off on the fateful journey which was to result in the destruction of the SIS's pre-war network of spies in Western Europe.

At the café Schellenberg and Alfred Naujocks, the chief of the squad of strong-arm men he had brought with him, waited nervously for their arrival. Naujocks, who will go down in history as the 'man who started World War Two',[12] was not happy with the set-up.

His men were posted in a car just beyond the red-and-white-striped frontier post. When the two Britishers appeared, they were to speed forward and snatch them. The driver would not attempt to turn, but would reverse immediately. At the same time other members of his squad would advance to left and right of the cobbled street to protect the flanks.

Naujocks was worried, however, about the possible reaction of the Dutch frontier guards to this breach of

[11] I am indebted to Herr Wolfgang Trees of the *Aachener Volkszeitung*, who interviewed Herr Lemmens, the last survivor of the 'Venlo Incident' for me when he was in Europe in 1973. Mr Lemmens, now seventy-five, ended the war in Oranienburg Concentration Camp. Some time after his release he emigrated to New Zealand where he lives now.

[12] A squad under his command, dressed in Polish uniform, broke into the German Gleiwitz Radio Station and broadcast inflammatory statements before leaving behind them dead concentration camp inmates dressed in Polish uniform. See *War in the Shadows* (Ballantine) for further details.

Dutch neutrality. The many recent scares at the Venlo section of the frontier had made them trigger-happy; shooting would be inevitable. And Alfred Naujocks had no intention of stopping one of those bullets. Neither had Schellenberg. He had already told the twelve men of Naujocks' detachment that he looked a bit like Captain Best. 'I am of about the same build, have a similar overcoat and also wear a monocle.' He wanted no mistakes made.

After lunching at Den Bosch, Best took over the wheel from Jan Lemmens. Stevens, sitting by his side, began to scribble down a list of agents who had to be got out of Holland if the Germans invaded.

'Better destroy that list before we get to the frontier,' Best said. 'I have a feeling that something may go wrong.'

'Of course,' Stevens said.[13]

They drove on. Just before four, they reached Venlo. On all sides it was clear that the Dutch were expecting trouble; there were troops everywhere and they were stopped twice. Secretly Best hoped the troops would send them back; his 'feeling of impending danger was very strong'.

But as they approached the café everything seemed peaceful enough. There was no one in sight save a green-clad German customs official leaning on the red-and-white-striped pole and a little girl playing ball with a dog in the middle of the road. Best reassured himself that 'during the First World War [he] had been to the frontier dozens of times like this; much closer too, for the café in Limburg where [he] used to meet people was half in Holland and half in Germany'.

Schellenberg had just ordered another coffee when he heard the sound of the approaching car. He dashed into the street and waved his arm excitedly, as if the General were inside the café. Best brought the car to a halt next to the kerb. At that moment there was the roar of a car accelerating wildly. Naujocks' black Mercedes, its hood thrown back, swung through the barrier. It was packed with 'rough-looking

---

[13] Lemmens never saw Best tear up the list. In all probability it ended in German hands.

men'. Two of them were squatting on the hood firing over the SIS men's heads with their machine pistols; others standing on the running-boards were shouting wildly and waving their pistols. Almost immediately four of them sprang out and rushed forward, crying 'Hands up!'

Tamely the two spymasters surrendered. Stevens just had time to whisper to Best, 'Our number is up, Best,' the last words he would say to his colleague for the next five years, when firing broke out again behind them. Best swung round. It was Lieutenant Klop running away, firing as he went. Best thought he 'looked graceful, with both arms outstretched—almost like a ballet dancer'. Then the four Germans holding them started firing and 'Klop seemed to crumple and collapse into a dark heap of clothes on the grass'.

The Germans prodded their captives in the back with their pistols and moments later they were across the border. The barrier closed behind them. The two surviving chief SIS operatives in Western Europe were in Nazi Germany.

At the HQ of the Reich's Main Security Office Heydrich was shouting at Best: 'So far you have been treated as an officer and a gentleman but don't think that this will go on if you don't behave better than you have done,' and threatened to hand him over to the Gestapo 'who are used to dealing with such gangsters and criminals; you won't enjoy their methods a bit'.

Stevens' deputy, Captain Hendricks, was still in radio contact with Schellenberg. Naively he assumed that his two chiefs had been captured in a Gestapo operation and that Schellenberg was a genuine resister. On 16 November, still unaware of what had really happened, he told his radio operator, Walsh, to signal Schellenberg, who had been given a British radio earlier on: 'We are prepared now as before to continue negotiations along lines previously agreed upon. Next meeting must await results of consultation with Premier Daladier of France. In view of what has happened, must proceed henceforth with utmost caution.' But Heydrich and Schellenberg were bored with the game now and Schellenberg ordered the following signal to be sent: 'Negotiations for any length of time with conceited and silly people are tedious. You will understand, therefore, that we are giving them up. You are hereby bidden a hearty farewell by your affectionate German Opposition.' The barb was in the message's signature. It was signed. '*The Gestapo*'.

Hendricks' radio operator acknowledged the message's receipt with a polite 'Thank you', adding, as was his custom, his name, Walsh.

The receipt of that same message in London, however, threw the SIS office into a state of near-panic. Menzies and Dansey realized immediately that their key network was destroyed and that—with one notable exception, of which we shall hear more later—they would soon not have a single agent in Germany.

Group-Captain Fred Winterbotham, chief of air intelligence, who happened to be in Menzies' office when the news came in, recalls that his chief's face was 'a shade paler than normal'.[14] In a shaky voice, almost as if he were speaking to himself, he asked: 'What the devil are we going to do now?'

Winterbotham shrugged. 'Bloody fools,' was his sole comment on the two unfortunate SIS men, who were now locked away in the Gestapo cells below the Prinz Albrecht Strasse HQ; for he knew that, although the Continental SIS was virtually destroyed, the organization possessed a new intelligence weapon which, if correctly developed, might affect the whole course of the battle of wits between Britain and Twelveland.

[14] Menzies was so shaken by Himmler's disclosure at this time of the whole SIS organization and his own name, plus those of his agents, that he ordered the details to be locked away in a safe and classified as 'most secret' even to the members of his own staff.

5

THE ENIGMA

The origins of what Winston Churchill called his 'most secret sources' in his own account of the Second World War—he never identified them any further—are to be found in Warsaw in early 1939. Some time that winter a disgruntled young Polish mechanic, who had just returned to his native country, contacted the Polish Secret Service, which had already established a link with the SIS.

The young mechanic had an interesting story to tell the Polish intelligence officers. Until very recently he had been working in Germany at the top-secret factory owned by the German *Chiffriermaschinen Gesellschaft Heimsoeth*, Berlin, which was run by a Dr Rudolph Heimsoeth and Frau Elspeth Rinke.

The factory had been working at top capacity producing a battery-powered portable machine set in a wooden box about the size and weight of an office typewriter. Soon, so the Polish mechanic believed, the machine would be supplied to every major German military formation down to the level of division as a means of encoding top secret messages. The machine's name was the Enigma. The intelligence officers pricked up their ears; they had all heard of the Enigma.

At 2.55 p.m. on Tuesday, 7 October, 1919, a Dutchman named Hugo Alexander Koch filed Netherlands Patent No. 10,700 for a *Geheimschriffmachine*.[1] Eight years later Koch sold the patent to a German named Arthur Scherbius, who lived in Dusseldorf. The latter, who was an inventor, moved

[1] Literally 'a secret writing machine'.

to Berlin-Wilmersdorf, where he designed a machine including 'multiple switch boards which connect each arriving lead with one of the outgoing leads and which are adapted to interchange this connection with great facility of variation'. Although Scherbius did not describe his machine any further in his application for a patent, it was clear that he had invented a rotor system for numeral encipherment. He called his machine the Enigma.

The inventor thought his machine had commercial possibilities and he began to market it, describing it on the illustrated sales promotion literature in English thus: 'The natural inquisitiveness of competitors is at once checkmated by a machine which enables you to keep all your documents, or at least their important parts, entirely secret without occasioning any expense worth mentioning. One secret, well protected, may pay the whole cost of the machine.'

But Scherbius's Enigma did not catch on. One year after Hitler came into power, his company was liquidated and its assets were transferred to the new cipher machine factory set up by two directors of the original firm, Dr Heimsoeth and Frau Rinke.

Hitler had already set about enlarging the old *Reichswehr* to an organization of 35 divisions, which would be trained to reverse the conditions set up by what he preferred to call the *Versaillesdiktat*; and those divisions would need an absolutely foolproof coding machine. Dr Heimsoeth and Frau Rinke had established their new firm at just the right time. Orders came flooding in from the new *Wehrmacht*. The Enigma was on its way.

Knowing about the top secret machine, the Polish officers naturally thought that the Germans would have taken stringent security precautions to guard it. But the young mechanic surprised them. Although the Germans had limited each workman to making just one part of the machine, he had kept his ears and eyes open. He told the Poles that he thought he could reconstruct not only the one part he had worked on but the whole Enigma!

For reasons known only to themselves, the Poles contacted the London SIS. The British acted at once and the young mechanic was smuggled out of Poland through

Danzig where he was shipped to Paris to be taken care of by Bill Dunderdale, the SIS resident there.

Dunderdale and his pretty American wife lived in high style in a flat near the Champ de Mars. In spite of having an attractive wife, Dunderdale, who had served a long time in Russia and spoke the language fluently, was a great skirt-chaser and had made many conquests among the wives of the Diplomatic Corps. But he was also a skilled operator, who had compiled a list of all known new Red Air Force squadrons, for instance, with the aid of a wizened, chain-smoking Czarist general who had found refuge in Paris after the Revolution.

Dunderdale installed the mechanic in the Latin Quarter and guarded him while he worked on a wooden model of the Enigma. It is often thought among old SIS hands that Dunderdale was the model for Ian Fleming's James Bond. At all events this real-life '007' kept the mechanic secure in his Parisian hideout until he had produced his machine which was flown to the SIS headquarters at once.

'The thing looked a bit like a wooden pianola,' one eye-witness recalls. But it impressed Menzies enough for him to order that the Poles should try to steal the real thing.

Again the Polish Intelligence Service went into operation, this time using a powerful Swedish spy-ring, run by the Warsaw manager of the big Swedish industrial concern ASEA, a man named Sven Norman. Together with the ex-Swedish military attaché in Berlin, Colonel Carl Herslow, now Consul-General in Warsaw, he had set up a network in Germany, using Swedish businessmen, some of whom spied for money, others because they hated the Nazis.

The Norman ring managed to steal a working model of the Enigma a month before the Germans invaded Poland. Immediately Menzies sent the long-time head of the Government Code and Cypher School (mockingly called by its members 'the Golf Club and Chess Society'), Commander Alexander Denniston, to collect it from Poland. With only a matter of days to spare the Commander arrived back in London with the machine.

Alexander Denniston, a small, tight-lipped Scot, had transferred from Osborne College, where he had taught German, to Naval Intelligence in 1914 on the outbreak of the First World War. There he moved into the celebrated 'Room 40' of the Admiralty Building, where the famed Zimmerman Telegram, which helped to bring the United States into the war, was cracked in 1917.

During the four years of war, the team of linguist-cryptographers in Room 40 had swollen to eighty, including the Rev. William Montgomery, who cracked the Zimmerman Telegram, and Monsignor Ronald Knox and his brother Dilly, who achieved similar if unrecorded success in his work with the Enigma in the Second World War. But when the war ended none of the great cryptographers wanted to stay on working for Naval Intelligence. At a concert held one month later they sang:

'While some say that the Boche were not beaten by Foch
But by Winston or Ramsay MacDonald
There are others who claim that the *coup de grâce* came
from the Knoxes (our Dilly and Ronald).

and ended with the assumption:

'No more delights like thee for us
But Denniston will *never*
Desert his solitary post
He will go on for ever.'

For Denniston had decided to stay in the business. Cryptography had become his whole life. His son Robin remembers him as totally immersed in his work, 'a very curious man with no ambition like Menzies. Bad-tempered, impatient, with no time for the snobbish Menzies, he was a great friend of Vivian's, although he thought him exceedingly stupid.'

Menzies cordially reciprocated Denniston's dislike of him, yet for nearly fifteen years the two men worked side by side in the gloomy Broadway Building, with Denniston—'the most secretive man I've ever known', according to his son— struggling on a shoestring budget until Admiral Sinclair moved his unit to an eighteenth-century manor house in

43

Bletchley, Buckinghamshire, at about the same time as the Enigma was brought to England.

It was there that the experts began their work on cracking the codes used in the machine. Their results were disappointing. With the aid of the Enigma, codes could be cracked, but it would take, so the experts calculated, exactly five months to break each individual intercept.

Menzies, hard pressed by the lack of intelligence coming out of Twelveland, was at his wit's end; the machine had promised success where human agents had failed. Then Winterbotham suggested: 'Well, what about a machine to speed up the process? If a machine can encode a message, can't another one decode it? Can't we invent a machine?'

Thus the great idea was born and passed over to the Post Office engineers to work on. The months passed. Information from Germany dried up almost totally. Menzies was desperate. After the Venlo fiasco, the authorities had imposed what the old SIS hands called 'the commissars' on him, three senior officers from each of the services, who were lodged in the Broadway HQ to check on his activities. 1939 gave way to 1940. Then in February of that year the first four *Luftwaffe* HQ intercepts were unscrambled by the combined efforts of the new Post Office computer, which was based on stripping a numerical additive from the enciphered code, and Denniston's experts at Bletchley.

Winterbotham, as Chief of Air Intelligence, took them to Medhurst, head of the RAF Intelligence, himself. Medhurst was discouraging. 'Can't use them,' was his comment. 'You'll have to do better than that.'

But in the next weeks, as the phoney war gave way to the shooting war, with the Germans launching attack after attack, the mesages which started to come from Hut Three on the Bletchley Park estate, where the deciphering was done, began to prove their worth. Although the intercepts were not yet foolproof and often intermittent, they knew that they often had the German High Command's intentions, as it were, on the breakfast table before the subordinate German commanders received them. With the aid of these intercepts, of which Malcolm Muggeridge said thirty years later, '[they] had the rarity value of the Dead Sea

Scrolls', they could out-think and hopefully outfight the enemy.

But overjoyed as he was at the success of the Bletchley operation, Winterbotham was still worried. In May, 1940, when France was overrun and Bill Dunderdale, with what was left of the SIS organization in that country, fled the Continent, he went to see Menzies.

C was in a queer mood that May. On the one hand Denniston, whom he heartily disliked, had achieved a great triumph at Bletchley; on the other, the new Prime Minister, Mr Churchill, no respecter of persons or institutions if they were failing him, was presently occupied setting up a new secret service: SOE—Special Operations Executive—an aggressive clandestine outfit, which was intended to carry the secret war back to Europe. And it was to be placed, not under his command, but under that of Dr Dalton, an Intellectual and a socialist to boot. It was obvious that Churchill had lost confidence in him and his organization.

When Winterbotham told him in his forthright way that, 'This can't go on. The whole op will be blown in a few months if we don't control it properly,' C agreed and suggested that he, Winterbotham, take over the security of the Bletchley operation.

Thus the second aspect of the tremendous intelligence scoop came into being—the shadow OKW[2]—which Winterbotham was to control until 1942 when Menzies decided he could safely entrust its command to one of his own cronies.

Starting off with one officer, a German linguist named Humphries, and three hand-picked sergeants, Winterbotham set up a German High Command through which all the messages received at Bletchley would be channelled and then sent on to a limit group of high-ranking officers, certain ministers and, of course, Menzies. It was a very modest beginning for an organization which eventually ran into thousands of officers and NCO's and spread all over the world. It was a tremendous operation and an overwhelming security success which, in spite of the thousands of people involved in it, has been kept secret from the general public to this day. Philby, the Russian spy in the SIS, who knew

[2] *Oberkommando der Wehrmacht*, the German High Command.

about the intercepts and used them to his own advantage, obviously did not fully understand the operation. Nor did Malcolm Muggeridge who, as a new recruit to the SIS, was taken to Bletchley in 1941 as part of his training, though he did find out that, 'By virtue of just knowing about them [the intercepts] I automatically came into the category of

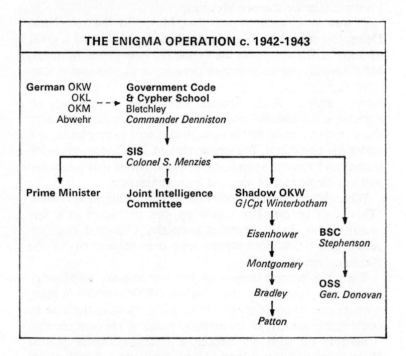

THE ENIGMA OPERATION c. 1942-1943

those who must in no circumstances fall into enemy hands for fear that, under interrogation or torture, I might be induced to disclose my knowledge, whereupon the enemy cipher would be changed and all the work of cracking it need to be done again.'[3]

Muggeridge gives the following picture of the members of Bletchley's Golf and Chess Club: 'mathematicians, dons of various kinds, chess and crossword maestros, an odd musician or two and numerous wireless telegraphy experts ... Each day after luncheon when the weather was propi-

[3] M. Muggeridge, *Chronicles of Wasted Time*, Collins, 1973.

tious, the cipher crackers played rounders on the manor house lawn, assuming the quasi-serious manner dons affect when engaged in activities likely to be regarded as frivolous or insignificant in comparison with their weightier studies. Thus they would dispute some point about the game with the same fervour as they might the question of free will or determinism or whether the world began with a big bang or a process of continuous creation. Shaking their heads ponderously, sucking air noisily into their noses between words—"I thought mine was the surer stroke" or "I can assert without fear of contradiction that my right foot was already..." '

But in the embattled summer of 1940 Bletchley's intercepts brought hope to those few in the know. They revealed that Hitler would not drive his panzers into Dunkirk, thereby allowing the British to plan the evacuation, which in that peculiar British way was seen as a victory and not as a defeat. The intercepts often gave earlier warnings of the massed German raids on London and the South Coast than did the radar which was officially revealed as 'the secret of our success' and the weapon which helped to win the 'Battle of Britain'.

About midday on a late September day, Winterbotham received information from Bletchley that the real OKW in Berlin had given orders to dismantle the aircraft loading ramps on a certain Dutch airfield. He realized immediately what that meant. Hurriedly he forwarded the news to the Chiefs-of-Staff, and added a note to the Prime Minister's copy, explaining its import.

Churchill reacted at once. He called a meeting of the Chiefs-of-Staff for that evening in his underground War Room and invited Menzies and Winterbotham. The relief, after the strain of the last few weeks, was tremendous; for the intercept confirmed that *Operation Sea-Lion*, Hitler's plan to invade south-east England was definitely off. As Winterbotham said later, 'The generals had funked it.' Churchill invited the high-ranking officers outside for a breath of fresh air. The mist had cleared and the warm September night was ideal for raiders. The *Luftwaffe* was now making full use of its opportunity. As Churchill emerged from the huge concrete screen in front of the War Room the night was loud with the crack of the anti-aircraft guns and the whistle and boom of the German bombs. London was afire but Churchill ignored the danger. Flanked by his Chiefs-of-Staff, his chin thrust out, his steel helmet set at a cocky angle, cigar clenched between his teeth, he stared at the scene of destruction in Whitehall. Then he took out his cigar and growled: 'We'll get the bastards for this!'

For Winterbotham this was indeed 'one of those piquant moments of history'.

PART TWO

DEATH COMES TO THE MAN WITH THE IRON HEART (1940–1943)

'After all, the whole Czech underground is financed and directed on the one hand by the British and the other by Moscow.'

'Gestapo' Mueller to General Schellenberg, 1942

1

THE RICKMAN LEAGUE

'We are divided from England by a ditch 37 kilometres wide and we are not even able to get to know what is happening there!' Hitler exclaimed angrily in 1941, though his words would have been equally applicable in 1940. His Intelligence seemed to know nothing of what was going on in Britain.

Apart from the rudimentary 'Shadow OKW' operation, which was still being developed, the British were little better off. Although on a clear day it was possible to tell the time through binoculars on Calais clock tower from the battlements of Dover Castle, the British knew virtually nothing of what was happening in German Occupied Europe. As Peter Fleming, the chronicler of Operation Sea-Lion, has written 'they [the Intelligence experts] were like insects deprived of their antennae'.[1]

As Colonel Bickham Sweet-Escott, a new recruit to the SIS, summing up the organization's record by the mid-summer of 1940, said, 'Our record of positive achievement was unimpressive. There were a few successful operations to our credit, but certainly not many; we had something which could be called an organization on the ground in the Balkans ... but as for Western Europe, though there was much to excuse it, the record was lamentable, *for we did not possess one single agent between the Balkans and the English Channel!*' Although the Colonel was not, strictly speaking, right—we did have one agent, as we shall see— there was *no* SIS organization left in western Europe. It was time, as Menzies realized, to rectify that fault—this time making his base of attack on Twelveland one of the

[1] P. Fleming, *Invasion 1940*, Rupert Hart-Davies.

two remaining neutral states in northern Europe, namely Sweden.

The opportunity presented itself through the person who was to become indirectly the founding father of the CIA, the 'Quiet Canadian', William Stephenson, undefeated world amateur heavyweight boxer, RFC fighter ace and multimillionaire inventor who owned factories all over the United Kingdom.

Stephenson, who had lived in England since his release from a German POW camp after the First World War, had been supplying Menzies with information about Germany's industrial strength for a couple of years prior to the Second World War. When Winston Churchill returned to the Admiralty in 1939, Stephenson suggested to him that the Swedish shipments of high grade iron ore from the Gallivare mines to Germany should be sabotaged. At the outbreak of war Germany had only enough quality ore to last for nine months and it was imperative that the Swedes kept supplying her. Churchill, always an addict of bold unconventional operations, proposed to the War Cabinet on 16 December, 1939 that the Swedish ore 'must be prevented from leaving by methods which will be neither diplomatic nor military'. The implication was clear. Churchill was suggesting that the SIS sabotage the Swedish ore shipments.

When Chamberlain approved, Stephenson volunteered to do the job himself. The matter was discussed with Menzies and he agreed, loaning Stephenson one of his operatives—37-year-old Alfred Rickman.

Rickman had been in Sweden during most of 1938 and 1939, apparently studying the mining of iron ore. (He actually published a book on the subject.) In reality, however, he had been working with a British advertising man named Ernest Biggs and an ex-communist named Ture Nerman. Together they published a pro-British paper in Stockholm called *The Front*, while at the same time flooding Twelveland with propaganda letters.[2]

---

[2] One of Nerman's authors was the late Chancellor of West Germany, Willy Brandt. (Nerman published his first three books.) Right-wing commentators in West Germany have maintained that Brandt worked for the SIS at some time or other in the last years of the '30s.

On 8 February, 1940, Swedish postal censors made a routine check on a letter addressed to a Herr Kutzner, Berlin, N.W.40, Post Office Box 23.

Dear Herr Kutzner,
Many thanks for the pen which Horst brought from you. I am using it for the first time and hope that you will be pleased with my use of it. The contact with Uncle Richard of which I've heard you speak has not been too successful up to now, but I think it holds promise for the future.

The old man is very suspicious and can't expect much from the contact with me. But I hope to get in touch with his family and in this manner win his confidence. Although he doesn't speak Swedish yet, he is already at home here and it's always interesting to observe a man carrying out his job . . .

One is happy to hear anything from the Old Country in both senses of the word. What do you think of my plans to make a move? I don't know if I can realize them. At all events I'd be grateful for your advice, which is important. Regards.

Yours,
Kant.

The Stockholm censors were so puzzled that they decided to submit the letter to a chemical examination. And thus they were able to read the letter's real message written in invisible ink. (Hence, presumably, the reference to the pen.) The message was as follows:

After some effort, I've been able to make out the representative of the Secret Service here. To do this, I made contact with an acquaintance, an emigrant in London. My guess that he had made similar contacts in England was not mistaken. I got in touch with him through a courier (English) and through him to a Mr Rickman, who is studying Swedish Ore and has written a book on the subject. This man is working for Mr Wilson[3] whose

[3] This was probably Jock Wilson, one of Vivian's men from the

53

acquaintance I have not yet made. He spends his time between here and Norway, where he is running a brand new department for sending propaganda into the Reich. He has his material franked with German stamps to be posted in the Reich.

The quality is lousy from what I have seen of it. I have an acquaintance working in this field who has given me some small insight into the business. Rickman is scared of the Swedish authorities and tries to conceal everything. At present his interest is concentrated on Mālmo. In the future I'll call him Uncle Richard in my reports. Perhaps I can get to England through him and his people. There I've got other contacts (press, Foreign Office). You'll hear from me further. Your respectful Kant.

When the deciphered message was handed to the Swedish Political Police they saw at once that they were dealing with a German spy, spying on British agents in Sweden. But what were the British up to? And who was Kant?

The cover name was not very profound.[4] The police investigators immediately thought of the celebrated German philosopher of that name, whose Christian name was Immanuel. They set to work searching through their lists of German immigrants to Sweden (or so they said later) and discovered that on 16 October, 1939, a journalist named Immanuel Birnbaum had entered on a German passport.

On 13 April, 1940, he was arrested. He denied writing the letter, but when the police found the invisible ink, he confessed that in the previous November he had received a visit from a fellow journalist named Wolfgang Horst who said he represented the Berlin *Zeitungskorrespondenzbuero*, for which he had himself worked before he had fled from Germany on account of being half-Jewish. Some time later,

Indian Police, who planned the assassination of Heydrich and later ran the Danish section of the SOE (1942–5). Jock Wilson was also a director of the International Boy Scouts.

[4] Today, when one reads the account of the investigation, it is apparent that the whole thing was a set-up job, with the Germans feeding the information to the already initiated Swedes who were basically pro-German, especially in official circles, until Germany started to lose the war, so that it would appear that the 'neutral' Swedes had discovered the SIS plot in a routine way.

at the bar of the Stockholm Opera, Horst had recruited him for the German *Abwehr*.

'Kant' was sent to prison where he remained until 1941, when he was freed, still protesting that it had all been a put-up job, while the Swedish police started hunting for 'Uncle Richard'.

The day before Birnbaum's arrest, Rickman, who was exceedingly nervous and insisted on carrying a revolver at all times, set off on his sabotage mission.

With him he had his secretary-mistress, Elsa Johansson, a German Social Democrat refugee named Arno Behrisch, to whom Rickman had promised ten thousand Swedish Kroner if their mission was successful,[5] and a Czech refugee named Rudolf Halbe. Travelling by train, they arrived at an island from which they could observe the Oxelsund port installations.

Rickman had plenty of plastic explosive with him and time detonators which would give them four hours to get clear before the bombs went off.

But the conspirators fell to arguing. Behrisch maintained that 'if we blow up the harbour installations, it could mean military intervention by the Germans and that would be a catastrophe for the Swedes as well as for foreigners like ourselves'. Rickman, well aware of Menzies' attitude to SIS funds, demanded his money back. Behrisch countered that he had given 3,500 Kroner to Halbe and, in addition, spent some of the money in 'expenses'. So the amateur saboteurs fell to arguing about money while the precious ore sailed unharmed to feed the roaring furnaces of the Ruhr. By now, helped by the German *Abwehr*, Stephenson's plan to blow up the installations had become the talk of the town. The Quiet Canadian feared that he might be murdered by the Germans, for as his biographer, Montgomery Hyde, wrote: 'There were plenty of German undercover agents in Sweden and they were quite capable of kidnapping or murdering the two British agents if they should discover what they were up to.'[6]

[5] Today Herr Behrisch is a highly respected back-bencher in the SPD Party.
[6] Montgomery Hyde, *The Quiet Canadian*, Hamish Hamilton.

The Germans had no need to go to such lengths. The amateurish plot was foiled more easily than that. Already they had helped the Swedish police to get on to the Rickman League, as the Germans were calling the plotters. Now they 'leaked' the details to King Gustav, who panicked, not because of the danger to the Swedish port installations, but because of his fears of a German invasion. He sent a frantic telegram to King George VI, asking him to call off his secret service. In his turn the British king lost no time in informing Lord Halifax, and the unfortunate Menzies, who set such faith by royal favour, was 'sent for'. Hastily the SIS dropped the operation.

Almost at the same time Rickman, his secretary-mistress, Biggs and Behrisch were arrested by the Swedish police and sent for trial. In June, 1940, Rickman was sentenced to eight years' imprisonment, Biggs to five and Behrisch and the girl to three. Ironically enough, the public prosecutor was the Swedish 'spy expert', Werner Ryhninger, who twenty years later was the prosecuting magistrate in the case of Sweden's super-spy Colonel Wennerstroem: the same Wennerstroem who in 1940 gave his *Abwehr* masters details of the Rickman League trial. A year later he changed his allegiance to the Soviets to become the most notorious spy in Swedish history.

The Rickman trial rocked the country and helped to make official Sweden even more anti-British. After all, the Germans were winning the war now! Thus, while the amateurish SIS agents went off to prison, Stephenson, the instigator of the whole thing, fled from Stockholm. Stephenson had never had much time for 'losers' and he had not been very impressed by Rickman anyway. As we shall see, his career with the SIS would eventually win him the coveted 'K'. But for the time being it was obvious that the organization's first attempt to carry the Intelligence war back into Twelveland had been a failure.

2

THE SWEDISH TRAVELLER

For a while the SIS operatives still remaining in Stockholm lay low. Now the only source of real information was a Swedish journalist of apparent Nazi sympathies named Ellsen and his friend, a Hungarian poster painter called Goroe. (They were both arrested in November, 1942.)

The job of obtaining intelligence from within Germany was taken over for a while by the naval attaché, Captain Henry Mangles Denham, who was also Naval Intelligence's representative in Sweden.[1] Although his key agent, a mysterious merchantman captain who sailed to the German Baltic ports, was really an *Abwehr* 'plant', Denham did make an interesting contact in the person of Colonel Bjoernstierna, head of Sweden's Combined Intelligence Bureau, and through him he obtained copies of the reports sent to Stockholm by the Swedish military attaché in Berlin, Colonel C. H. Juhlin-Dannfelt.

Menzies was grateful for the information he received but the material *was* coming from a service which he regarded as a dangerous rival. The wartime DNI was filled with bright, imaginative, young men who, among other things, pulled off the smartest deception trick of the whole war, the 'Man Who Never Was'. Nor had Menzies forgiven Naval Intelligence for Ian Fleming's attempts to poach Cotton from the SIS. In 1939 it had given him some malicious pleasure when, at the outbreak of the conflict, Admiral Godfrey, the new head of Naval Intelligence, had been forced to

---

[1] Captain Denham's greatest claim to fame is that it was he who first alerted the Admiralty that the *Bismarck* had passed into the North Sea and thence into the Atlantic on its way to that fateful confrontation with the Royal Navy.

telephone the Broadway HQ to state that the Admiralty's new chief, Winston Churchill, was breathing down his neck, wanting to know where the German fleet was.[2]

Indeed, Menzies was suspicious of Godfrey himself. Persistent rumours floated around the department that the Admiral, who was no enemy of good living—'he was an inveterate bottom-pincher', one female associate of the SIS recalls. 'None of his Wrens were safe from him'—*had a German-born mistress!*

At all events, Menzies ordered that a potential agent, who had been approached as early as 1939 by, of all people, the US Minister in Moscow, Ambassador Sterling, and left 'to sleep' ever since, should be activated. His name was Erik Erickson, one of the most successful yet most controversial spies in the employ of the SIS and, later, OSS.

Of Swedish descent Erik Siegfried Erickson had been born in Brooklyn in 1889. After graduating from high school he worked in the Texan oilfields until he had saved enough money to enrol as a student at Cornell University. His studies were interrupted by a short term as an officer in the First World War, but in 1921 he graduated in engineering. Then, at the age of thirty-three, Erickson set off on his travels, working as a salesman for various American oil companies and picking up a knowledge of French, Spanish, Japanese and Italian, in addition to the fluent Swedish and English which he already spoke. In the late 'twenties he set up in business for himself, making his base in Sweden and renouncing his American citizenship to do so. But he still kept on travelling.

In December, 1939, Laurence Sterling, the US Minister in Moscow, who had come to Stockholm to meet the Russian and Finnish representatives of a commission which had been sent to the neutral capital to see if they could work out some sort of compromise peace to end the Russo-Finnish 'Winter-War', enrolled Erickson as an agent.

At dinner in a Stockholm hotel, Sterling, who had been

---

[2] Winterbotham's pilot, Niven, had managed to supply that information, taking with him a West End passport photographer, who 'was scared out of his wits' and photographing the German fleet from over the Dutch border before Messerschmitt fighters scared him off.

briefed on the importance of oil in the German war effort, asked Erickson if he would try to re-establish his old business contacts with that country and in the course of his travels pin-point industrial targets. Sterling added that the information Erickson obtained would be passed on to the SIS.

Erickson agreed and, if we are to believe his own statements, though there were many business associates of his at that time who attributed other motives to his actions thereafter, he set about deliberately wooing the Germans. Thus, early in 1940, he set about transforming his image as a democratic American Swede into a pro-Nazi collaborationist businessman. He wasn't alone in his endeavours. Prince Carl Bernadotte of the Swedish royal house had also been approached by Sterling during his visit to Stockholm and asked if he would like to go to Washington. Prince Carl agreed and in 1940 he left for the American capital, where he was received by Cordell Hull and President Roosevelt. Prince Carl said he was prepared to help the United States and after meeting Lord Halifax, now British Ambassador in Washington, he agreed to supply both countries with information about Germany.

Prince Carl Bernadotte and Erik Erickson then used the cover of the Prince's Belgio-Baltic brokerage firm to obtain an entry permit into Germany for Erickson. It took some time but finally, in September, 1941, the American-Swede, who was now regarded as a German fellow-traveller among those Swedes who supported the British, was ready to depart for Berlin.

After Prince Carl and Erickson's new wife, Ingrid, had seen him off at Bromma Airport, Swedish detectives boarded the waiting *Lufthansa* plane and demanded to examine his luggage. Erickson protested hotly, but the detectives, who belonged to the pro-German Secret Police, insisted.

Erickson could not help thinking that his mission had been betrayed before it had started and with some trepidation he made his way to Gestapo HQ in the Prinz Albrecht Strasse to present his credentials.

The Gestapo officials knew of the Bromma airport incident already, but dismissed it as having been instigated by 'British agents' and Erickson was allowed to set off on his planned tour of the German oil brokers from whom he proposed to buy oil for Sweden.[3]

Most of the businessmen he intended to visit were well known to him from pre-war days and he had a pretty shrewd idea which of them might be prepared to collaborate with him. After all the oil business was an international affair and many of the Germans he was to visit had received their training in the USA or United Kingdom and, indeed, many of them had been employed by the US and UK oil giants.[4]

In Berlin he recruited his first agent, a German descended from an East Prussian Junker family, who, after working for an international oil factory, had volunteered to work for the German Petroleum Commission, which directed oil and petrol rationing and production throughout the Reich. But he had one condition to make—he wanted a paper from Erickson stating that he had worked for the Anglo-Americans during the war. Like most of the Germans Prince Carl and Erickson recruited throughout the war, he wanted to be on the winning side, whoever won the war. In spite of the obvious danger if the Gestapo ever discovered the document, Erickson signed his 'insurance policy', as the German called it.

In the week that followed Erickson looked up several prominent Germans whom he had known before the war and succeeded in recruiting two of them for his network, among them a minor oil executive and a banker who had interests in the oil industry.

From the latter Erickson found out that the Germans were going to rely to a great extent on their own synthetic oil industry if their supplies from Ploesti in Rumania were cut off. It was vitally important, therefore, for him to find out more details of synthetic oil plants located in the Hanover, Karlsruhe and Leipzig areas; and the place to do that

[3] At this time Sweden relied on Germany for most of her oil.

[4] In some cases, they were still employed by US firms, some of which were very pro-German. When Hess's plane came down in Scotland and the suggestion was made it should be put on exhibition to raise money for the British war effort, the PM had to veto the suggestion because both its fuel and tyres came from US firms. The American ITT built the Focke-Wulf which was shot down in large numbers over the UK by Spitfires equipped with ITT-built electronic equipment!

was the centre of the German petroleum industry, the seaport of Hamburg.

Ten days after his arrival in Berlin, he set off for Hamburg where he recruited a useful agent, a director of the Hamburg's *Vereinsbank*, a position which gave him access to Hamburg's *Prominenz* and through them to the men who ran most of Germany's refineries. Again Erickson was foolish enough to entrust the man with a certificate stating that he was working for the Anglo-Americans.

Thus, within a matter of two weeks, Erickson managed to build up a small but valuable network of agents, who were shrewd enough to cover both sides of the field in order to protect themselves in the post-war period. Satisfied, he flew back to Stockholm and presented his report to the US Embassy there, from whence it reached the SIS HQ in a matter of a few days.

The Secret Air Intelligence branch, which had been under Winterbotham's command until he moved to the 'Shadow OKW', analysed it thoroughly before passing on their findings to Bomber Command, where it was filed away for further use. For the time being 'Bomber Harris's' men could do little with Erickson's information. They hadn't the long-range planes to make use of it.

In six months' time Erickson's initial trip would, however, help in the planning of a raid of which the official history of the US Air Force in the Second World War would write:[5] 'Despite the modest result, the strike of 12 June was as significant as any the AAF had flown in the six months since Pearl Harbor. It was the first American mission in World War II to be levelled against a strategic target.'

It was the famous American raid of 12 June, 1942, on the Rumanian refinery at Ploesti.

[5] *Army Air Forces in World War II.*

3

THE MAN WHO KNEW HIMMLER

On the same day that Erickson was driven to Number 8, Prinz Albrecht Strasse to be checked by the Gestapo, the head of that organization arrived in occupied Prague with a staff of sixty-two 'specialists' to take over the post of Deputy 'Reichs Protector'.

The 'Protector' of occupied Czechoslovakia, the old-school diplomat, Baron von Neurath, had failed to get the nation which had given birth to the arch 'lay-about', the Good Soldier Schweik, to work efficiently for the German war machine. Now the dynamic 37-year-old Heydrich had been given the job. As he had explained to his pregnant wife, who had burst into tears on hearing the news, 'I'm doing something positive now. I'm sick of getting rid of people, putting them behind bars. This is my chance to do something with purpose.'[1] Heydrich plunged eagerly into the new job. His policy was the well-tried one of 'sugar and the whip'. While raising Czech rations, instituting the first 'health clinics' and rest homes, he also had two hundred intellectuals executed within the first week.

But as October gave way to November his policy began to pay dividends. Production in the Skoda factories, now working for Germany, rose, while resistance to the Occupation fell as more and more of the intellectual leaders were arrested and executed. The reports filed in London by the SIS's key agent in central Europe, code-named 'A 54', began to give ever more alarming details of the progress being made by the dynamic new master of Prague.

[1] Frau Heydrich to the author. She had told her husband previously that she would 'never see him again'. Her words were soon to come true.

By 1941 'A 54', the 'man who knew Himmler', had been spying on his native country for five years with ever increasing success. But in February, 1936, when he had first made his badly-written approach to the Czech Intelligence Service (it was so full of spelling mistakes that the Czechs could not believe its writer was a German), the Czechs had been inclined not to accept his startling offer, feeling that it was too good to be true; it must be a 'plant'.

As Lieutenant Alois Frank of the Czech Intelligence Service recalls: 'The letter caused a sensation. A German wanted to give us information about German intelligence coming out of Czechoslovakia, the German espionage set-up in the country . . . and demanded 15,000 marks in German currency for his services. He wanted the first four thousand marks by next week. He also needed a camera for the job, which he would buy in Germany for security reasons. Finally he let us know that he would break off all contact with us for a year after the delivery of the first batch of material . . . He would wait until 14 February for our answer and it depended upon this answer whether or not he would offer the material to the French Intelligence Service. The letter was signed "Your FM" with the address FM 137, poste restante Annaberg/Erzgebirge.'

The head of Lt Frank's department called an immediate conference, where the various possibilities were eagerly discussed. Finally the officer in question, Lieutenant-Colonel Frantisek Moravec, decided they would reply that day, sending the 4,000 marks, giving as a cover name and address: 'Karl Shimek, Dostal Lane, Prague'.

FM's reply was not very encouraging. He gave a few names of German agents working with Czechoslovakia and those of their contacts within the Reich. But still Moravec was confident that they could get more out of him. He wrote back and suggested that he and Frank should meet the German on Monday, 6 April, 1936, at 8.30 p.m. at a lonely crossroads near the village of Weipert on the Czech-German frontier.

Thus the Czechs met the mysterious FM. As Frank remembers: 'Suddenly he appeared. Slowly and carefully he approached us. He gave the code word "*Altvater*" and went with us to our car. We drove to Komotau where we conversed with him for three hours. He told us his real name was Jochen Breitner and for security reasons he had not brought his papers with him. Apparently he worked for the Dresden station of *Abwehr* as an artist-photographer. Through his fiancée he had contact with *Abwehr*'s central registry. He also had access to secret material. He only offered his services to us because he wanted to pay his debts and marry in the near future.'

He had brought much more interesting material with him this time, including the organization of the German *Abwehr* and his network of agents on the border and within Czechoslovakia itself.

Moravec and Frank gave him a severe cross-examination and, in the latter's words, 'he exhibited the quickness and expertise that could only be possessed by the trained agent'. That night he was engaged by the Czechs as an agent and given the code-number A 54.

Soon A 54 became the best agent the Czechs had. A young Lieutenant named Frantisek Fryc took charge of him. Although Fryc met him several times in 1938, the German remained very much of an enigma. Once he told the Czech: 'I hate the SS—I hate them like the plague.' Another time he maintained that he had Slavic blood in his veins, also that his mother came from the Lausitz district.

On 3 March, 1939, Lt Fryc met A 54 for the last time at Turnau. A 54 got down to business at once. As Fryc recalls: '[He said] the final decision has been made in Berlin. Czechoslovakia will cease to exist by 15 March at the latest!'

The young officer immediately informed Moravec who passed the word on to the Czech government. He also went to see the SIS resident in Prague and arranged with him to have the Czech Intelligence Service's secret papers transferred to London as well as some of its staff.

On the same day that the Germans marched into Czechoslovakia, eleven senior intelligence men landed at Croydon in a KLM machine by courtesy of the SIS. The SIS's security was not too good, however, for the *Daily Mail* reported their arrival, and in the March 15 edition of the paper there is a picture of three of the Czech intelligence men peering out of the plane's window above a headline which reads 'Eleven Mystery Men Arrive By Air, Sign Secret Register'. On that same day a certain Dr Paul Hans Steinberg registered at the Hotel Golden Goose in Prague's Wenzel Square. Agent A 54 had arrived in the country for which he had been spying these last three years. The question now was whether he would be prepared to continue spying for a nation which no longer existed and whose intelligence service was really an off-shoot of the SIS?

In the month that followed their arrival at the Grosvenor Hotel, the eleven spymasters quickly took up their old occupation. Colonel Moravec remained in London as head of the Czech Intelligence Service while Lt Fryc went to Paris, where he operated from a villa in the Avenue Victor Hugo and Frank went to The Hague to a cover job provided for him by the SIS in the British coal-import firm Foster & Co.

Almost immediately after his arrival Frank went to visit a Czech couple named Jelinek who ran an antique shop in the centre of the capital. The Jelinek shop was a cover for the Czech Intelligence's collecting centre in Holland, and Frank knew A 54 had its address. On 13 April, 1939, he received by postcard the first indication that A 54 was going to continue spying for the Czechs.

Some time later he arrived in The Hague personally to meet not only Frank but also Stevens and Best, a meeting which was to serve one day to put the final nail in his coffin. At the meeting held in the Jelinek home, it was agreed that A 54 should be given a new cover-name—Franta—and that the Czechs could write to his girl-friend's address, which was beyond suspicion, especially if Frank continued to write to him with his special secret ink—milk!

Franta proved a Godsend, especially when information dried up almost completely in Twelveland. He sent Lt Fryc in Paris a message via Switzerland in which he revealed the complete German invasion plan for France. (The French General Staff refused to believe the information.) He informed London that Operation Sea-Lion had been postponed. He was one of the first to radio (he had now made contact with Czech resistance which possessed a transmitter) that Germany was going to attack Russia, though the SIS already knew about this from its Bletchley intercepts.

As President Beneš recorded in his memoirs: 'From the beginning of April, 1940, we received daily information from absolutely unimpeachable sources in Prague and Berlin.' The Prague source was A 54, alias Dr Steinberg, alias Franta, alias Dr Holm, plus all the other names which Jochen Breitner, as he had called himself at that first meeting, had a fondness for. But who was he in reality?

His real name was Paul Thuemmel, a baker by trade, who had been born in 1902 at Neuhausen on the German side of the Erzgebirge Mountains. At the age of twenty-five Thuemmel had founded the local branch of the National Socialist Party and to celebrate the event he invited one of the Party's *Prominenz* to come and speak to the new members. The man was Heinrich Himmler!

That meeting was the start of his amazing career in intelligence. Himmler stayed the night in Thuemmel's mother's home and soon the two young men were using the familiar 'thou' to one another. They corresponded, and met when Thuemmel went to Bavaria on Party business. In 1933 Himmler obtained a post for Thuemmel in Admiral Canaris' *Abwehr* and he was posted to the Dresden branch of the German intelligence service, where he served for three years before offering himself to the Czechs, presumably for money.

It is difficult to understand why he continued to serve them after 1939. Did the Czechs threaten to blackmail him? Or did he, as an old SA man, genuinely hate the SS who had broken the power of the SA in 1934 after the so-called Roehm Putsch? Or did he really feel an empathy with the Czechs as fellow Slavs? We shall never know. However, in the years 1940–1 he was able to warn London of the Schellenberg attempt to kidnap the Duke of Windsor in Lisbon and of the German plan to invade Jugoslavia.

The Gestapo had long been after the heads of the Czech resistance movement, more especially as they had learned that the Czechs were in radio contact with London. More than once they just missed the head of the radio group, who once smuggled himself into Prague's Gestapo HQ and wrote on a wall: 'I was waiting for you, Fleischer. Where

1. Captain Stewart Menzies (second from left, rear rank) when on Haig's Intelligence staff during the First World War.

2. Sir Stewart Menzies in his role as 'C', the head of the British Secret Intelligence Service.

3. *Der Seekadett*—Canaris as a cadet at the beginning of a career that brought him the rank of Admiral and the leadership of the Nazi *Abwehr*.

4.   Frank S. Cotton with Air Marshal Sir Arthur Barratt.

5.   Prince Carl Bernadotte (right) with Erik Erickson.

6. Group-Captain Frederick Winterbotham, Chief of Air Intelligence and subsequent head of shadow OKW.

were you?' The reference was to Commissar Fleischer, who had set up a trap to catch the elusive Czech.

But on 3 October, 1941, Fleischer and his colleagues captured the Czech transmitter and a hoard of valuable material which indicated that there was a high level traitor within Germany's own ranks. The new Deputy Reich Protector was informed immediately and Heydrich formed a special search squad for the unknown traitor who was now code-named 'Verraetter X' (Traitor X). The squad, which established itself in an office in Prague's Wenceslas Square, soon discovered that 'Traitor X' lived somewhere in the north of Prague. But where? It was a large area with a couple of hundred thousand inhabitants. But the search squad had two very special men among its members: Commissar Will Leimer and Commissar Nachtmann, both of whom had already infiltrated the Czech underground movements. They had wormed their way into the resistance movement directed by the exiled Czech government in London and were busily betraying its members to their colleagues. They were also deeply involved in the communist Czech resistance and similarly engaged in betraying Gestapo secrets to the Czechs. For both the Gestapo commissars were long-time NKVD agents![2]

Nachtmann and Leimer were both, understandably, regarded as 'red' experts and in their first months in Prague they had dutifully helped to arrest the Czech communist opposition, which, prior to Germany's attack on Russia, was regarded in Moscow as a danger to the new friendship between the two countries. On 'Gestapo Mueller's' orders, for instance, they had taken part in the arrest of a 37-year-old communist councillor from the Prague suburb of Karlin, of whom the world would hear more later. His name was Antonin Novotny. He was sent to the concentration camp

[2] The two German traitors, who worked for the Russian Secret Service organization, carried out their amazing game throughout the war. In 1944, for instance, a Czech SOE agent, who worked as a secretary to the head of the Prague Gestapo, warned the London-orientated Czech resistance that they were in danger. Its head immediately informed one of his most trusted men, 'Lt Sulc'. In his turn, Sulc betrayed the SOE agent to the Gestapo. 'Sulc' was of course Nachtmann. The girl was executed.

at Mauthausen, where he became a *Kapo* and waxed fat while another obscure communist from his own country named Stefan Dubcek waned exceedingly thin, losing over four stone in weight.

On 22 June, 1941, however, when Germany attacked Russia, the two traitors were ordered by the Russian 'resident' in Prague, General 'Konsul', to support the local communists. At the same time they also had to further Russia's long-term territorial aims, which included domination of central Europe. This would mean the liquidation of the London-run Czech resistance movement and their mainstay, Paul Thuemmel.

Indirectly Paul Thuemmel was already known to them. After the French General Staff had paid so little attention to his warning of the German attack through the Ardennes, A 54 had begun to doubt his 'case officers' in London and their British masters. As a result he had made a preliminary approach to the Russians through the Czech resistance movement. It was an approach that was now to prove fatal for him. The communists passed on his name to the two NKVD agents. They ensured that their colleagues of the 'Traitor X' squad obtained it. Thus it was that Thuemmel, betrayed by the new allies of his masters in London, was arrested on 13 October, 1941.[3]

Thuemmel tried to justify his actions by saying that he had really been working as a double agent. He had been planning a big coup when he was arrested; he had been attempting to capture the whole Moravek network, which ran the radio link with London.

On 2 March, 1942, he was released on his 'word of honour' with the promise that he would attempt to arrange a meeting with the elusive Moravek. Once he did so, but only after he had warned him what was afoot. Moravek went

[3] My informant on the strange three-sided game being played out in Prague in 1941, Major 'F', recalls that in 1962, seeking information on the Thuemmel affair on behalf of the Czech government, he wrote a formal letter to the Soviet KGB. A month later he was informed that their files on the subject had been burned in a fire in 1950. However, one of his Czech colleagues, head of Section V, whose cover name was 'Majer', told him that Colonel Litvinov, the KGB liaison officer in Prague, had told him, Majer, that Leimer was now a colonel in the Moscow HQ of the KGB.

to the appointed meeting place but left before *Kommissar* Fleischer appeared, leaving behind him an unpleasant sign of his contempt for the Gestapo—his faeces and a note saying: *'Keep this for the Winterhilfe'*.[4]

In the meantime Thuemmel contacted London through Moravek and pleaded with his 'case officer' to send a plane to rescue him; he knew that the SIS was regularly flying planes into the heart of Czechoslovakia to drop supplies and parachutists.

But that wasn't to be. Thuemmel was rearrested and Heydrich wrote an urgent letter to Martin Bormann, head of the Party Chancellery, asking if Paul Thuemmel, 'holder of the Party's badge of honour, Party Number 61,574' could be expelled from the NSDAP because he had worked for 'the Czech-British Secret Service and received at least 40,000 Reichsmarks for his treachery'.

Bormann, now the 'brown eminence' of the Party, wrote by return that Thuemmel had been expelled though 'neither he nor Party Headquarters for the District of Saxony' would be informed.

Willi Abendschoen, Thuemmel's last interrogator, soon cut through the agent's final lies. He recalled that during the interrogation of Best and Stevens in Berlin they had mentioned a high-ranking German who had come to visit them in The Hague in 1939. He checked back and found that on the date in question Thuemmel had stopped by the important *Abwehr* post in Muenster on his way to The Hague. It was the only break on his journey to that fateful meeting in the Jelinek house.

A few days later, Thuemmel was given the last of his many aliases. As Major Peter Toman, 'the former Dutch military attaché in Prague', he was sent to Theresienstadt concentration camp and thus passes out of this story.[5]

But although the main character had disappeared, his story did not end there. Six weeks after his delivery to the

---

[4] The German relief organization for poor people to help them over the winter.

[5] Surprisingly enough he survived until 20 April, 1945, Hitler's last birthday, when he passed through the camp 'door of death' to die at the hands of a firing squad.

concentration camp, Reinhard Heydrich summoned a conference of the senior officers of his own Reich's Main
Security Office and Admiral Canaris and his aides to
Prague. The case of the *Abwehr* traitor was to be used to
humiliate the little white-haired spymaster and play a part
in Heydrich's plan to amalgamate all German intelligence
services under his own command.

At 10.30 a.m. on 18 May Heydrich appeared with Canaris.
Heydrich made the opening speech. Canaris followed it with
one suggesting that there should be closer co-operation between the *Abwehr* and the Main Security Office, a proposal
that must have caused Heydrich no small measure of inner
mirth.

The Admiral was followed by the chief of the Gestapo,
Heinrich Mueller—'a decent little man', Best called him
after Mueller had interrogated him several times in the
Prinz Albrecht Strasse. The ex-Bavarian policeman, who
had persecuted both communists and Nazis with equal fervour in his days as a police detective in Munich, did not
hide his contempt for Canaris's *Abwehr*. He stated point-
blank that the Canaris organization was old-fashioned and
bureaucratic. The Admiral's eyes revealed nothing, but he
could not conceal his emotions when at the end of the conference Heydrich enumerated his conditions for further co-
operation between the Reich's Main Security Office and the
Abwehr. 'Heydrich's Decalogue' or the 'Ten Comman-
dantments of the Prague God', as they were called later, were
harsh and brutal: 'Because of the situation at home and
abroad, the organization and personnel of the *Abwehr*
must be changed. The present officers of the *Abwehr* have
shown they are incapable and they must be replaced by new
men, trained by the SS. In the interests of Reich Security,
there must be a centralized secret service organization. Its
representatives would have the power to act in all departments and to draw on the total manpower. These men would
be responsible to their Minister, to the Minister of State—
and to me!' It was the writing on the wall for the *Abwehr*.

It was clear to the Admiral that the days of his organization were numbered. But Canaris need not have worried.
Nine days later Reinhard Heydrich, so confident that he had

tamed the Czechs that he had dispensed with a bodyguard, was mortally wounded by Czech parachutist agents, while driving through the suburbs of Prague. He died eight days later, his plan to centralize the secret service organizations unrealized.

It is often said that Heydrich was assassinated by the Czech parateam *Anthropoid*, which included the two killers Jan Kubis and Josef Gabchik, because his régime had increased Czech war production and taken the sting out of the Czech resistance organization. Yet when the mission was originally planned by the Czechs in August, 1941, the target was not Heydrich at all. In a secret radio message to 'Jindra' [Professor Ladislav Vanek, head of the Czech resistance] the exiled Czech President, Eduard Beneš, informed him that the team intended to assassinate either the German State Secretary, Karl Hermann Frank, or the symbol of treason in occupied Czechoslovakia, the Education Minister, Emanuel Moravec. This message was sent nearly seven weeks before von Neurath was recalled and Heydrich appointed in his place. When the target was changed to Heydrich, 'Jindra' protested to Beneš. He pointed out, rightly, that reprisals could be expected.

President Beneš said that he agreed that the assassination of Heydrich was not in the best interests of the Czech nation but that the exiled Czech government in London was under pressure to carry it out. Indeed, when the killers were finally flown into occupied Czechoslovakia it took them six months to carry out the assassination, throughout which time 'Jindra' tried without success to get Beneš to cancel the operation.[6] Who, then, insisted on the killing and why? When Jan Kubis and his friend Josef Gabchik dropped over Czechoslovakia in December, 1941, Thuemmel's reports

[6] I am indebted for this new light on the Heydrich assassination to Major 'F', a Czech defector from the Main Directorate of the Czech Intelligence Service, who worked for seventeen years in its Prague HQ. During the course of his research into the career of a triple agent who landed with the *Anthropoid* team, he went through the thousands of documents dealing with this period, which still rest in Prague's Snemovni Street, the HQ of the present-day Czech Intelligence.

had not yet revealed the success of Heydrich's policy. Why then the switch from Moravek, whose murder would not have occasioned massive reprisals, to Heydrich, whose murder did?

According to my informant, 'the decision to assassinate Heydrich was taken under the pressure of the British Intelligence Service. The SIS was afraid that its contacts with the *Abwehr* officers would be swept away if Heydrich realized his plan to unify the Nazi Intelligence Service, the SD, with the *Abwehr* under his leadership.'

But who could those contacts in the *Abwehr* be? Not Thuemmel, for he was already compromised and the SIS did not lift a finger to save him. Was it the group around Colonel Oster in the *Abwehr* HQ, who were actively plotting against Hitler and who, as we have seen, actually gave secret information to the British via Colonel Sas in 1939? But by 1941 the SIS had lost all real contact with Oster and Menzies wanted nothing to do with the German resistance. After playing with that particular fire at Venlo, Menzies did not intend to be burned a second time; and, as we shall see, it was this refusal to do business with the German resistance which cost him the services of the greatest spy in the German camp in 1943—Wood.

Now we do know that the SIS played a great role in planning the assassination. It was Colonel Wilson of the SIS who trained the *Anthropoid* team in northern Scotland. It was the SIS which provided the Canadian-crewed Halifax which flew them in; and it was the SIS which vetoed any attempt by post-war researchers to rattle that 'well-stocked morgue of bones for historians', as Alan Burgess put it,[7] in order to find out details of Kubis' and Gabchik's careers in the United Kingdom.

But why? Not for the sake of any contacts within the *Abwehr* but because the SIS wanted to show the world the power of its long arm, its ability to strike back against the man who had humiliated them so deeply at Venlo two years before!

To the very end 'Jindra' pleaded with the two killers to

[7] See Alan Burgess, *Seven Men at Daybreak*, Evans Bros, for further details.

give up their attempt, but they were adamant. 'A complicated situation had developed. Kubis and Gabchik wanted to carry out the assassination come what may,' he said after the war, 'although our organization had been in difficulties since the end of March, 1942, due to the loss of a radio operator and several of our people. But every time I attempted to explain the consequences of their deed, they answered obstinately that they had their "orders" and they would carry out their task sooner or later.'

As we know, 'Jindra' failed and the world soon learned of the full extent of the Germans' terrible revenge. Baldur von Schirach, Gauleiter of Vienna and three-quarters American (his grandfather had been a Civil War general in the US Army), urged that an English town of some cultural value be destroyed as a reprisal. But Bath or York were saved another 'Baedeker raid'.[8]

The full wrath of the Germans was turned on Czechoslovakia. Some 1,331 Czechs, 201 of them women, were summarily executed and ten thousand sent to the concentration camps. Lidice was wiped out and the name entered the terrible history of Second World War horror and terrorism. It was, however, one of the greatest propaganda victories of the Western Allies in the course of the war. A Mexican and an American village changed their names to Lidice and a film was made of the event which was shown in most neutral countries.

Menzies' elimination of Heydrich, regardless of the cost to the Czechs, made a tremendous impression on the Germans.[9] Schellenberg, the head of the SD wrote; 'The assassination certainly had its effect on the work of the

8 In May several British towns, such as York, which had no military importance were bombed by the *Luftwaffe*. Having been at the receiving end of those bombs I can testify that one of those towns at least had no defence whatsoever.

9 If we are to believe the Czechs, the SIS had deliberately interfered in Czech affairs prior to the war in order to break up the country and force Germany into an eventual conflict with Soviet Russia. It is known that Colonel Christie of the SIS had several meetings with Conrad Henlein, the head of the Sudeten German movement, which eventually asked Hitler to take over their area of Czechoslovakia. Indeed Heydrich had Henlein shadowed when he went to Switzerland to meet Christie. But so far there is no proof that Henlein was a British agent and naturally the SIS will not open its files.

central office in Berlin. Instead of the hum of intensive activity, there was a hush of incredulity, almost of fear. How could such a thing have happened?'

It needed Schellenberg to find the answer to that question. Admiral Canaris was also quick off the mark. Although Canaris broke down at Heydrich's funeral and turned to Schellenberg and said: 'He was a great man. I have lost a friend in him,' he made an immediate overture to Menzies.

Through his contracts in Spain, Canaris suggested that C should meet him in neutral Libson. It was a proposal which makes the mind boggle, but C was ready to fly to Portugal to meet his opposite number, whose career he had studied carefully for over half a decade. Conservative and straight-laced as he was, Menzies was intrigued by the German admiral, who was reputed to have been Mata Hari's lover and to have killed an Italian priest in order to escape from prison while under sentence of death for spying. He knew too of the admiral's ambivalent attitude to Hitler, of his strange restlessness, his constant travelling, his devotion to his two dachshunds and his delight in cooking and his North African chef Mohammed.[10]

Eagerly C forwarded Canaris' proposals to Anthony Eden, the Foreign Secretary. But Eden vetoed the meeting. He told Menzies that he might well be kidnapped; after all Schellenberg had already kidnapped two of his men in neutral Holland and had attempted to do the same to the Duke of Windsor in Portugal.

But that was not Eden's real reason. Britain now had a new ally, Russia, and those new members of the 'great fight against tyranny' were battling for their lives; it would not look well if the Russians discovered that a meeting was taking place in neutral Lisbon between the heads of the two enemy secret services.

Thus Menzies was denied the opportunity to meet Admiral Canaris. He was 'very disappointed', but all the same he must have been very satisfied that summer with the results of that meeting so long before at the border cross-

---

[10] On New Year's Eve, 1942, for instance, Canaris donned a chef's hat and apron and cooked the dinner for his staff at a Spanish outpost. One can hardly imagine the head of the British SIS doing the same!

roads between the two Czech intelligence officers and 'the man who knew Himmler'.

Now as the first defectors from the *Abwehr* started to surrender to SIS agents in Turkey, Spain, Switzerland and Portugal, Menzies knew that his organization was winning the battle for Twelveland. The time had come to lend a hand to the erstwhile Russian allies. But the 'Bolsheviks', as he called them privately, would have to be helped by the SIS in a strange way. Without their knowledge. The greatest deception of the Second World War's war in the shadows was about to begin.

PART THREE

THE ENIGMA VARIATIONS
1942–43

'There'll always be a Bletchley
As long as there are bricks
So here's to every billeter
And every billetrix.'

> *Wartime amateur dramatics*
> *production, Bletchley, Bucks.*
> (Sung to the tune of '*There'll*
> *always be an England*')

1

DORA, SISSY, LUCY—AND OTHERS

Five months after the German surrender at Stalingrad, on 1 July, 1943, Adolf Hitler laid down the final date of the German summer offensive which he hoped would reverse the effects of that defeat. *Operation Citadel*, which would be launched on the Eastern Front in the region of the city of Kursk, would begin on 5 July.

On 2 July, a pudgy bald Ukrainian political commissar with the Red Army, who held the rank of Lieutenant-General and was one day to become the leader of the Soviet State, called together the commanders of the Voronezh Front. In a wooden hut located near the village of Sorin-skoya Dvori, General Nikita Khrushchev told the Red Army officers: 'The fascists will attack between the third and fifth of July. That is no guess. *We know it for certain!*'

On 5 July, 1943, just as he had predicted, forty-two German divisions, assisted by 3,000 tanks, attacked. Twelve days later, after they had run into massive, prepared resistance which decimated the panzer divisions leading the drive, Hitler called off the great offensive. It had been a total failure.

Almost immediately, with that German penchant for blaming others for their failures, the High Command suspected treachery; the Russians had obviously been waiting for them. Colonel Teske of the Central Army's transportation organization, said, 'They must have had early notification [of the objective]. Both collection areas were the target of severe disruptive attacks from the middle of March onwards.' General Halder, Hitler's Chief-of-Staff until 1942, went even further. In an interview with the German magazine *Spiegel*, twenty-five years later, he maintained that

'Nearly all German attack plans were betrayed to the enemy through the treachery of a member of the Führer's headquarters before they even landed on my desk. We were unable to plug this leak right up to the end of the war.'[1] Little did the general know that in the final months of the war he was very close to two men who might well have told

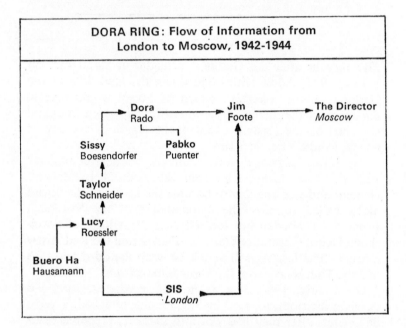

DORA RING: Flow of Information from London to Moscow, 1942-1944

him the name of that hidden traitor; for he was imprisoned with Best and Stevens. But he never discovered.

Both Teske's and Halder's suspicions of treachery were later confirmed by an intercept picked up by the *Abwehr* listening post at Stuttgart. When it was finally deciphered, it read:

27 May, 1943. To the Director. Urgent!
1. All preparations have been made by Army groups von Kluge and Manstein to move all their motorized units from the second line to the front ready for action. These troops will be in their jump-off positions by 1 June.

[1] *Der Spiegel*, 1967

2. The German High Command intends to undertake a limited attack on the Southern Front in the first days of June. The Germans want to use this attack to show the Russians that Germany is not concerned by the situation in the West and that Russia must fight on alone for the time being. In addition the German High Command is concerned with achieving new victories in order to encourage the Army and the German people.

The message, from the illegal transmitter located somewhere in Switzerland, was signed 'Dora'. Its source was given as 'Werther, Berlin, 23 May'.[2]

It was clear to the cryptographers in Berlin who broke the message that the Russian High Command was receiving information from a communist spy-ring located somewhere in Switzerland, which had an agent somewhere right at the top in the Führer's HQ. That summer the frustrated *Abwehr* and their colleagues in Mueller's Gestapo, who had just successfully broken up one great Soviet spy network,[3] must have sweated blood in their efforts to find out who 'Werther' was.

Werther's story started almost ten years before in 1934 when a small, sallow German named Rudolf Roessler crossed the Swiss border into exile.

Roessler had been born in Franconia in 1897, the son of a civil servant living in Augsburg. At the age of seventeen he volunteered for the Imperial Army and served on the Somme and in Flanders with a Bavarian Infantry Regiment. He wasn't a particularly good soldier—he was never promoted and failed to win even the Iron Cross, third class, at a time when the decoration was handed out in thousands.

He was glad to return to civilian life in 1919 and took up journalism on the editorial staff of his hometown newspaper

---

[2] This was naturally only the first of the messages which allowed the Russians 'not only to detect the general concept of the attack, but also its probable direction and the forces to be used'. (*The History of Great Fatherland War of the Soviet Union*, the official Soviet war history.)

[3] The Red Orchestra network, led by Leopold Trepper, a Polish Jew, which stretched from Sweden to Belgium. Ironically enough Trepper had first organized it with the UK as its 'target country'. It changed its 'target' when Germany attacked Russia.

the *Augsburger Allgemeine*. Ten years later he had become the general secretary of the *Buhnen Volksbund*, an association of theatregoers in Berlin. By this time he was a staid solid citizen whose politics, on the whole, were left of centre.

But Hitler's take-over in 1933 brought a radical change in his life. A year later he voluntarily went into Swiss exile, one of the many thousands of exiles who were crossing Germany's frontiers westwards. The frontier guards passed him without much comment and he received his residence permit almost immediately. For there was nothing significant about Rudolf Roessler—no burning fury at the injustice of it all, no over-riding determination to take his revenge on the Nazis, nothing to indicate that he would one day become the Soviet High Command's main source of information—the chief architect of the great victory at Kursk!

He seemed a perfectly ordinary person to those who knew him at the time. The German historian, Ritter von Schramm, who had known him in the 'twenties said: 'It was and still is for me a huge problem how this man ever became an intelligence agent . . . He was the typical German dreamer.' The Swiss Intelligence officer, Hans Hausamann, with whom he worked, said of him later: 'Roessler wasn't the spy type at all. It would be a great mistake to compare Roessler with Sorge (the great Soviet spy in the Far East).'

For the next five years Roessler's behaviour did not deviate in any way from the pattern of life which he had established hitherto. He earned his living, not a very good one, by republishing the works of writers banned by the Nazis—books by people such as Paul Claudel and Stanley Baldwin—at his Vita Nova Publishing House in Lucerne.

In July, 1939, however, Roessler made contact with the semi-official Swiss intelligence organization built up by the wealthy St Gallen photographer, Hans Hausamann. Hausamann had tried to make up for the deficiencies of officialdom by setting up his own intelligence group for, as he said after the war, 'it was simply my duty as a citizen to protect my country and I could do that by accelerating the downfall of Hitler'. In spite of his German name and the close proximity of his home to the German border, his intense dislike of the Germans motivated him to set up '*Buero Ha*' or '*Pilatus*', an organization which became part of the official Swiss intelligence service upon the outbreak of war. Thus Roessler, who began supplying Hausamann with snippets of information, usually picked up from German visitors and German newspapers, indirectly became part of the Swiss official intelligence network.

That same month Roessler put an advertisement in the *Neue Zuercher Zeitung*, the country's leading German-language paper, for a man with a good general educational background. Almost immediately he received an answer from a certain Dr Christian Schneider.

Schneider was, like himself, a German in exile, who had earned his living since he had been expelled by working as a translator in the League of Nations Organization at Geneva. As the discredited League was now cutting back on its staff, Schneider jumped at the opportunity of working for a fellow countryman.

Thereafter Roessler began to send Schneider a weekly batch of instructions to his home in Geneva, often enclosing little notes which contained some military secret. After war broke out these notes grew to such an extent that Schneider's wife asked him once, 'How can Roessler know anything like that?'

Schneider's reply was, 'Roessler has confided to me that he has good sources in Germany.'

That remark was the only statement he ever made about the source of his information.

But Schneider was also working for the Russian intelligence service!

The Soviet spy-ring in Switzerland had been organized prior to the war by a bespectacled Hungarian cartographer named Sandor Rudolfi who, when he entered Switzerland in 1936, had changed his name to 'Rado'. Born in Ujpest in 1888, the son of a Jewish businessman, he had become a communist in a Red regiment during the short-lived régime of the notorious Bela Kun. After its failure he fled into exile, becoming an undercover agent for the Comintern in 1921. In the years that followed he carried out assignments for the international communist organization throughout western Europe. At the same time he was able to complete his university career, open a publishing business and establish an international reputation for himself as a cartographer, publishing the world's first travel guide to the USSR, the first air travel guide and a number of essays—all written by himself—which occasioned the British Royal Geographic Society to invite him to become a corresponding member.

In 1935 he returned to Moscow on business where he was approached by the then head of the Russian Secret Service, Semjon Urizki, who asked him to accept an important post in the Russian organization. He told Rado who by now spoke six languages fluently, 'I'd like you to be quite clear about the aims and tasks of our job. First of all we've got to decide who will be our probable enemy and then begin our intelligence work. As you know the Soviet Union has many potential enemies in Europe. But our primary enemies are Germany and Italy. Now let us decide where you will settle—I know you speak several European languages—and what your cover will be.'

Thus it was that Rado set up a small printing house in Geneva in May, 1936 (after failing to obtain a residence permit for Belgium), which would finance the spy-ring by the sale of maps and sketches to newspapers.

For the next three years Rado led a quiet life, in the course of which he built up three small spy networks in Switzerland.

The first was run by a socialist journalist named Otto Puenter, whose ring was code-named Pabko after the residences of his chief agents—Pontresina, Arth-Goldau, Berne, Kreuzlingen and Orseling. The second, code-named Sonia, was led by a German communist Ursula Kuczynski, who was married to a Soviet agent, Rudolf Hamburger. This group employed two recently recruited veterans of the International Brigade, who had successfully escaped from Spain, the radio operators Alexander Foote ('Jim') and Bill Philips ('Jack'). The third group, Sissy, was directed by a Polish Jewess, Esther Boesendorfer, who was now a Swiss citizen and employed as a typist in the International Labour Office; and it was 'Sissy' who one day was going to recruit Roessler through the agency of Schneider whose not very profound cover-name was 'Taylor', the literal translation of Schneider into English.

From 1939 to 1941, the Dora network, as the Soviet spy-ring in Switzerland was called, did very little. As Foote recalls in his *Handbook for Spies*, 'I used to look back wistfully on the pleasant pastoral interlude while the war was still static and Switzerland, as an intelligence centre, moderately static.'

All that changed on the morning of 22 July, 1941. At 4.45 that day 'Jersey's'[4] tanks crossed the River Bug and the life-and-death struggle between the two dictatorships had begun. That same afternoon, Rado, the least martial of all the great spymasters of the Second World War, composed an aggressive message 'in the name of all my comrades' for the Director in Moscow. It read:

'In this historic hour, we promise to fight on at our forward post with unshakeable loyalty and redoubled energy!'

Then he went over and had a Scotch with 'Jim' in his flat. 'Dora' had gone to war at last!

In the first months of the new war it was Otto Puenter,[5] an ex-Austrian Social Democrat official, who was the most successful supplier of secret information about 'Jersey'. In 1940 Puenter had made contact with a disgruntled ex-member of the French *Deuxième Bureau*, who went under the code-name of 'Long'[6] and had built up excellent contacts in Berlin before the war when he had been a journalist there for *Le Journal*.

One of his most important contacts there, code-named 'Agnes', later came to fame in post-war Germany, serving as a conservative minister for nearly ten years. He was Ernst Lemmer, a 43-year-old ex-member of the German *Reichstag*, who had lost his post in 1933. In that year, as he records in his memoirs, he went to Paris to look for work. 'But the couple of days I spent in Paris at the end of May sufficed

---

[4] Soviet Intelligence's equivalent to 'Twelveland', their code-name for Germany.

[5] He is still alive. Today he is a district judge in Berne.

[6] The French Intelligence officer, who used journalism as his cover before he was expelled from Germany just before the war, was probably Georges Blun.

... to make me decide to stay in Germany and accept all the risks of personal danger.'

In other words he had been given employment by the French Secret Service. Thereafter he also obtained employment with a supposedly independent information bureau for foreign newspapermen, which, in reality, was financed by the German Foreign Office. The Bureau turned out to be a splendid source of both political and military information for 'Long' and later for Puenter (as well as the Swiss Intelligence Service, for Lemmer supplied them with intelligence too.)[7]

On 27 October, 1941, for instance, Rado radioed Moscow:

A member of Ribbentrop's Office (I'll call this source 'Agnes') reported by telephone from Berlin to the editor of the *Neue Zuercher Zeitung*.

1. The tanks of the propaganda companies are waiting at Brjansk for the drive to Moscow. The date of the drive was supposed to be 14 October, then 20 October.

[7] In all fairness to ex-Minister Lemmer it must be stated that he denied all contact with the 'Pabko' network after the war. In an interview with *Der Spiegel* (16 January, 1967) he claimed from his hospital bed that 'I would have died of fear' if he had been connected with spying in any way. His only surviving relative, ex-Secretary-of-State Gerd Lemmer, had no comment to make when questioned on the subject of his uncle's apparent wartime activity by the present author. However, West Germany's Conservative governments of the 1960s contained one minister who had spied for the Russians and one state secretary who had been engaged in clandestine work for the British. When the Socialists came to power, they could boast of a senior adviser to Chancellor Brandt who had been a Soviet spy and a man who had tried to infiltrate the OSS after the war; a minister and chief party ideologist who had actually been jailed for spying for the Soviets and an assorted number of MP's who had worked for the British, Russian and probably also the American intelligence agencies, and, in one notorious case, were still working for such a spy organization.

The case of Herr Steiner, the Conservative MP whose one vote, which he did not give, would have tumbled Chancellor Brandt from power in 1972, has just come to light. According to Steiner's own confession, not only did he spy for the French *Deuxième Bureau*, but also for the intelligence agencies of both West and East Germany. One could almost conclude that espionage is virtually a second career in German politics.

More recently the sensational discovery that one of Chancellor Brandt's senior advisers, Herr Guillaume, had been an East German spy for more than twenty years caused a major governmental crisis and forced Chancellor Brandt himself to resign.

2. On 17 October new instructions were given out in case the siege of Moscow took longer. Heavy coastal artillery and artillery from the Maginot Line and Koenigsberg has been on its way to the Moscow Front for several days now.

   The German Press has been ordered not to report the 'Battle for Moscow'.[8]

But Lemmer was not the only source in Berlin available to the Puenter-Long team. There was the Swiss newspaperman, Dr J. C. Meyer, who like Lemmer, had represented the *Neue Zuercher Zeitung* in Berlin until he was expelled from Germany at Easter, 1940. Thereafter he became a sergeant-major in the Swiss Intelligence, running a whole group of informants in Germany. They included a Berlin industrialist who was a close acquaintance of General Keitel and the Reich's Press Chief Dr Dietrich, an SS major working in the Air Ministry, a general in the SS and director of the Munich Metal Works, a general without a command, a quartermaster in the High Command, the managing director of a large southern German factory, a senior official in the Foreign Office etc. *And all their reports received by Meyer in Switzerland eventually found their way to Rado!*

Indeed, if one surveys the list of informants in Germany in 1942 who were betraying their country by espionage either from opportunism or genuine opposition to the Hitler régime, one might well make out a case that Hitler was stabbed in the back in the Second World War by the same professional middle class which had put him in power nearly ten years before.

But it was, surprisingly enough, Sissy which made the first major intelligence breakthrough when Dora went operational in 1941 and provided Rado and Soviet Intelligence with the greatest and most successful agent they ever had. On the morning of 17 June, 1941, Sissy called Rado on the telephone. She was very excited and asked her boss to come over at once, for she had just received an important piece of news. Rado went to her apartment and was told

---

[8] It must be pointed out that in his own account of the 'Dora' network Rado himself identifies Lemmer as 'Agnes'.

that the information came from a Swiss who had just returned from a business trip to Germany. Her news was indeed of the greatest importance and Rado encoded it and ordered 'Jim' to send it to Moscow at once.

It read: 'On the Soviet-German border there are about one hundred infantry divisions, one third of them motorized. In addition there are 10 tank divisions. In Rumania troops are concentrating near Galatz. At present élite divisions are being alerted for special duties.'

The Dora organization had received its first indication of the German attack on Russia.

A couple of days later Sissy rang him again and gave him the exact date of the attack on Russia—22 June, 1941. She also told him that she had received the information through Taylor, who Rado knew had no contacts whatsoever with 'Jersey'. Where, then, did Taylor get his information?

Rado was immediately suspicious. 'His information,' as Rado wrote later,[9] 'which Sissy passed on to me, was concrete and so detailed that we wondered whether or not someone was smuggling false information to us through Taylor. We found it strange because this man, a simple translator in the International Labour Office, had no means of obtaining information of a military nature. Up to now we had neither expected nor received valuable information from him, and we were surprised that he had suddenly started contributing such extraordinarily valuable material. News of this kind, if it had been known to the enemy, would have caused consternation in the German General Staff.'

A valuable new source of information had been tapped by Rado. By the time the Dora network was finally broken up by the Swiss police the still unknown source's massive supply of information dominated the whole ring. 'Lucy', as Rado subsequently code-named him, had entered into the great game.

[9] S. Rado, *Dora Jelenti.*

2

WHO IS WERTHER?

In 1942, while Taylor continued to supply such vital information, the anonymous and 'usually exceedingly cautious Director' (thus Rado) decided that he, Taylor, should be put to the test. He asked Rado to tell Taylor to try and discover the number of German POWs held in Russia and the individual formation numbers of the German units fighting on the Southern Front.

Within two days, Taylor supplied Sissy with the required information and on 13 August, 1942, Rado radioed the Director:

'On 1 May the following units were fighting on the southern sector of the Eastern Front: Tank Divisions—the 7th, 11th, 14th, 16th and 22nd; Motorized Divisions: the 18th, 60th, 70th' etc.

Taylor also gave the number of German POWs in Soviet hands as 151,000.

These figures were obviously correct and the Director radioed back his satisfaction with their mysterious new contact man. In November of that year, when the Germans and the Russians were preparing to fight the decisive Battle of Stalingrad, Taylor came to Sissy, and told her that his 'German friend' was now ready to supply Soviet Intelligence regularly with top secret material.

According to Taylor, Lucy had been supplying the British with material on the events in Russia via the Swiss Intelligence. But now he was disgusted because the British had tossed it unused into their wastepaper-baskets.

As Rado writes in his book: 'Taylor informed Sissy that he and his friend were prepared to help the Soviets without any payment of any kind save their costs. . . . However

Taylor made one condition. *His friend would work with us only if we made no attempt to discover his true name, his address and profession* (author's italics).'

After 'serious consideration' the Director in Moscow accepted the conditions, warning Rado, however, to tell Sissy not to reveal her true identity either. Thus at the end of November, Lucy began working full time for Rado.

As the months passed he began to dominate the whole network with his information. Rado could not cope with the encoding alone and now empowered Jim (Foote) to encode as well as transmit of his own accord, an important point to bear in mind. To cover up his own inherent laziness, and make himself seem more important in the Director's eyes, Rado also invented a whole ring of German informants who supplied Lucy with top secret details of what was going on in Berlin. There was 'Olga', for instance, the code-name for the *Oberkommando der Luftwaffe*, the Air Force HQ; 'Anna', who worked in the *Auswartiges Amt*, the foreign office; and 'Teddy', 'Ferdinand' and 'Stefan'. But Lucy's key agent was 'Werther', who spied in the *Oberkommando der Wehrmacht*, the Army's HQ, and it was 'Werther' who was to enter the mythology of espionage as the *'grosse Unbekannte'*—the great unknown—in the German High Command, who was to present such a puzzle for writers from half a dozen nations after the war, not to mention the intelligence services of those same countries. All of them, amateurs as well as professionals, were to ask the same question: who was Roessler's chief contact in the German High Command? *Who was Werther?*[1]

In the meantime the Germans had not been idle. They had picked up their first two messages from the Dora network at midnight on 6 September, 1941. Although they could not decipher them, they did discover they were numbered 207 and 208. From this they drew the conclusion that over two hundred messages had already been sent by the Soviet transmitter on Swiss soil. Canaris and Schellenberg were informed

---

[1] The name might well have been taken from Goethe's famous eighteenth-century novel *The Sorrows of Young Werther* which caused such a suicide craze among Europe's young romantic discontents at that time.

and the nearest listening post at Stuttgart was ordered to locate the Swiss transmitter.

It took the radio detector experts months. Because of the topography of western Switzerland from which the messages were coming, it was hard to pinpoint the exact location of the transmitter. However, after some hard work, the Germans located the three illegal stations in Switzerland, operated by Jim, a married couple named Hamel, and Rado's mistress, Margit Bolli, a plump dark-haired cashier working in a restaurant. They named them 'die roten Drei'—the 'red three'.

Angry at this evidence of Soviet spying in their backyard, the Germans began to put pressure on the Swiss in the person of the head of the Swiss Intelligence Service, Colonel Roger Masson.

Since the war Masson, who later became a brigadier, has been portrayed as a man who was ruined because of his pro-Allied sympathies. (He was court-martialled and retired in September, 1945, on account of his role during the war when he was decorated by both the British and the Americans.) But in 1942 he did not seem so sure about an Allied victory. At all events in the late summer of that year he accepted Schellenberg's offer to meet to discuss the situation of a captured Swiss spy who was in German hands.

But that wasn't his real reason. In reality he was concerned about the potential threat to Switzerland posed by the Germans and thought he would pump the head of the *Sicherheitsdienst* on the subject.

But when the two intelligence chiefs met in the southern German border town of Waldshut, the young SD General, who was prepared to ruin Masson if necessary, easily outsmarted the older man. By dropping hints that the German General Staff were considering plans to invade Switzerland, he ensured Masson's co-operation; and the latter's desire to co-operate grew even greater in the following months.

Of course, Schellenberg knew that Hitler had no intention of invading Switzerland, although there was a contingency plan for an invasion in the files in Berlin. But by March, 1943, he had worked up Colonel Masson to such a state of alarm that the latter even convinced the Commander-in-Chief of the Swiss Army, General Guisan, to go with him to meet Schellenberg at the border village of Biglen. Here the SD General demanded a written guarantee of neutrality from them. With this, so he assured the two hopelessly outclassed Swiss officers, he could make the Führer drop his invasion plans.

They agreed, even to the key sentence that read: 'The balance of power in Europe demands a Switzerland which is neutral to all sides and in every respect.'

The way was now open for the anti-communist Swiss Federal Police—'the Bupo' (short for *Bundespolizei*)—to take a hand in the hunt for the 'red' transmitters, aided first by a renegade German Jew, Ives Rameau, whose real name was Ewald Zweig, and who was a Gestapo spy.

By this time too, one of Schellenberg's men, a ladies' hairdresser named Peters, had become the lover of Margit Bolli, Rado's mistress. He had forced her out of Rado's bed into his own and had began to pump her systematically for information. By the beginning of November, 1942, 'Romeo', as Peters was aptly code-named, knew everything that was going on at the fringes of the Dora network. In March, 1943, he managed to steal her decoding key and pass it on to the SD, who after decoding many of Margit's messages, passed on the information to the Bupo.

But the Bupo's hands were tied by the regulations which stated that espionage was the business of Army Intelligence, and they already knew that Captain Waibel and his right-hand man, Mayr von Baldegg, of Army Intelligence, were somehow mixed up in the game.

Then chance took a hand. On the night of 11 September, 1943, a young Army signals officer named Maurice Treyer picked up a strange transmitter while on duty on the shore of Lake Geneva. He guessed it was illegal and reported his suspicions, not to Intelligence but to the Bupo.

The police officer did not enlighten him on his mistake. Illegal transmitters were their province; and Inspector Marc Peyot, an anti-communist skilled in decoding, ordered Treyer to keep up his search for the illegal radio.

On 20 September, Treyer located the Hamel station. Five days later he pinpointed the one operated by Margit Bolli.

On the night of 13 October, 1943 both groups of operators were arrested by the Bupo, '[and] after we realized that we were dealing with a large scale spy organization,' Peyot said after the war, 'we decided to let the third transmitter, which we had discovered was located in Lausanne, continue working . . . He was working with a different code than Rado and we could not crack it. Then suddenly to our great surprise Foote . . . started to use Rado's code which we could read.

'His messages dealt with the agents already arrested in Geneva and led us to conclude that Rado had suggested he should continue his activities under the protection of the British Embassy in Berne.[2] But we did not allow that—not only because Moscow rejected his proposal, but also because, after an attempt which failed, we caught Mr Foote in flagrante.'

It was almost, as another police officer said at the time, 'as if Mr Foote wanted to be caught as well as having his message about Rado's intended approach to the British known to the world.'

Thereafter the Dora network was rounded up one by one, all save Puenter and Rado, who both went underground. Thus by the end of May, 1944, Foote, Taylor and Lucy were in jail, though none of them served a long sentence.

In January, 1945, Foote flew with Rado to Moscow, where he was appointed a captain in the Soviet Intelligence Service, while Rado, for his part, was sentenced to twenty-five years in a Soviet labour camp for having approached the British. But Foote did not stay long in the Soviet service. As soon as he had the opportunity to go west, he defected from East Berlin and returned to England.

Roessler was not so lucky. Eighteen months after his release, an old acquaintance from his wartime days turned up again in Berne—'Uncle Tom', who had worked for the SIS as a liaison man with Captain Hausamann's 'Buero Ha'. Now he was *Major* Sedlacek, the Czech Military Attaché to Switzerland, and he wanted Roessler to spy for him again.

---

[2] Rado was to pay dearly for that proposal with ten years in a Russian slave camp, his reward for his long service in Switzerland. In 1955 he returned to his native country and became a professor of geography.

And Roessler agreed. But it was poor stuff he delivered to his new masters, bringing him in the equivalent of twenty cents an item. Apparently he did not have the access to old sources in Germany, the country that 'Uncle Tom' and, later, his Soviet masters wanted information about.

In the end the Swiss, who had been watching him all the time, were forced to arrest him yet again. At his trial he pleaded that US policy in Germany had been 'to mobilize the historical bearers of imperialism and militarism'. The Swiss press, which had been roused against him prior to the hearing, was impressed by his obvious sincerity and his idealism, which one witness testified had been 'naive and unreal'. It applauded the judge's decision to let Roessler off with the mild sentence of one year's imprisonment.

But Roessler, who will always be regarded as one of the 'stars' of twentieth-century espionage, never recovered from that sentence. Five years later he was dead, taking the secret of his sources in the Third Reich with him. Taylor was already gone, soon to be followed by his son, to whom Taylor had confided Roessler's great secret, killed in a motor accident.

Today the bones of Rudolf Roessler lie under a simple gravestone in the cemetery of the little Swiss town of Kriems, five kilometres from Lucerne, and the stone above them with its legend 'Rudolf Roessler 1897–1958' gives no clue to the fact that here is buried the greatest intelligence enigma of the whole of the Second World War.

3

JIM

He was 'a burly, genial, humorous Englishman, whom I got
to know in his last years when he was working in one of the
Government departments.' So Malcolm Muggeridge remembers Foote after his 'defection' in post-war London. 'He
would drop in for a glass on his way home and we had many
laughs together comparing the fatuities of British and Soviet
Intelligence Services.'

At those meetings in the years just before Foote's death,
Muggeridge, studying the ex-deputy head of the Dora spy
network, 'never had the feeling that he was capable of revolutionary fanaticism or especially interested in revolutionary
doctrine. He was just a nice, easy-going man who was caught
up momentarily in the gale and whirlwind of our time and
then thrown back into the quiet waters of Ag. and Fish.'
A decade before, Foote's nominal chief, the Hungarian
Rado, had felt the same: 'My impression of Alexander
Foote was rather mixed. Undoubtedly he was intelligent and
possessed a strong will. He was humorous and inclined at
times even to irony . . . His education was limited and he had
not learned a profession. But the thing which surprised me
most was his complete lack of political education. This
man, who was so talented in technical and money matters,
had great difficulty understanding the international situation
and he had only a very vague understanding of the workers'
movement. One example: on 7 November, 1942, the 25th
anniversary of the Great Socialist October Revolution,[1] I
arrived at his flat in Lausanne with a bottle of champagne to

[1] The Russian Revolution of 1917.

celebrate. I suggested we should drink a glass in celebration, whereupon he looked at me questioningly. It turned out that he didn't even know what the day was and the importance of it for us and the whole of humanity!'

So much for the political convictions of the Englishman, who had given up everything to fight in Spain against the fascists and had abandoned his own country to spy for a foreign power.

Alexander Foote had been recruited into the Soviet espionage set-up in London. On a pleasant October day in 1938 Foote knocked on the green door behind which the Russian contact was waiting for him.

'You will proceed to Geneva,' he was told by 'the respectable housewife with a slight foreign accent' who interviewed him, where he would be met 'by a woman carrying a string shopping bag containing a green parcel'. She would also be holding an orange in her hand.

Foote, whose vaguely sketched-in biography in his book *Handbook for Spies* gives absolutely no reason why he should have got into the underground activity, duly met his contact outside the Post Office in Geneva and was recruited into the Swiss network by Sonia, his new boss. As Muggeridge wrote: 'If ever the day comes when there is no woman similarly accoutred outside the Geneva GPO we shall know that the intelligence services of the world have been disbanded and the millennium has come!'

Sonia, or to give her real name Maria Schulz, who was married to a Red agent under arrest for espionage activities in China, was a veteran spy herself. 'Slim with a good figure and even better legs,' as Foote described her, she was a determined and purposeful woman who first sent Foote and a fellow recruit 'Jack' or Bill Philips, another Englishman who one day was to become Sonia's lover, to Germany to study the situation there and learn the language.

But in Munich Foote's espionage career nearly came to an end before it started. It was part of his training there to keep an eye on Hitler; but after a couple of months the Director in Moscow decided that he and Bill Philips should assassinate the German dictator.

Foote did not like the idea one bit. With that overriding

cynicism of his which belied his supposed revolutionary zeal and idealism, he said later: 'Neither of us really fancied a martyr's crown ... We did feel, however, that in fairness to our employers, who, after all, had been paying us for some months with little or no return for their money, it behoved us to look into the matter—and the result was not un-promising.'

The two amateur assassins knew the restaurant where Hitler lunched very well. Usually he ate in a private room which was only separated from the corridor which led to the lavatories by a thin wooden partition. What would be easier than to leave a briefcase containing a bomb in that corridor and hurry out to wait for the bang.

But first they decided to test out the Führer's security. One day they were waiting for him as he entered, followed by his entourage, which they imagined would include 'a fair sprinkling of trigger-happy Gestapo agents'. Bill, seated at a table next to the gangway, rose as did the rest of the guests as the Führer entered; then slipped a hand furtively into his pocket—and drew out a cigarette case!

Foote, waiting tensely for any reaction, watched in vain, although 'to my heated imagination no action could have looked more suspicious'. Nothing happened. Hitler passed on his way.

Fortunately for Foote, however, Sonia could not provide the necessary explosive suitcase, and Hitler was saved, to become the assassination target, not only of the British SOE and the American OSS, but also of his own *Abwehr*; and like the Russian Secret Service, all of them failed.

'With such innocent sports,' as Foote wrote later, he and Bill Philips whiled away the time in Munich until their recall to Switzerland in 1939. Thereafter Foote led an easy life until 1941 when, as we have seen, Dora became the key Soviet network in Western Europe.

Like the members of the world's oldest profession, those who belong to the world's second oldest, spies, are usually lazy. Rado, Foote's chief, was no exception. As 1941 gave way to 1942, he burdened his deputy and radio operator with more and more work. In 1942 he found a convenient excuse to empower Foote with the encoding and transmitting of all key messages. Thus it was that Foote encoded and sent most of Roessler's reports for Moscow when Lucy began to work full-time for the Russians.

And what messages they were, if we are to believe Foote, who positively gloats over the work of this man about whose identity he is so coy: 'Lucy provided Moscow with an up-to-date and day-to-day order of battle of the German forces in the East. This information could only come from the *Oberkommando der Wehrmacht* itself. Not only did he provide the day-to-day dispositions on the Eastern front, but also Lucy could, and did, provide answers to specific questions. It frequently happened that Moscow had lost sight of such and such an *ersatz* division. An inquiry was put through Lucy and in a matter of days the answer would be provided, giving the composition, strength and location of the unit in question.'

Foote goes on:

'If Lucy had confined himself to producing information regarding the German Army, that would have been in itself sufficiently remarkable, and as such he could have amply justified himself in the Soviet eyes. But his sources went further. Not only did he provide information on the troop dispositions, information which could only have come from the OKW in the Bendlerstrasse, but also he produced equally good information emanating from the headquarters of the Luftwaffe and the Marineamt, the German Admiralty . . . the possession of Lucy as a source meant that they [the Russians] had the equivalent of well-placed agents on the three Service Intelligence Staffs, plus the Imperial General Staff, plus the War Cabinet offices.'

Foote ends his hymn of praise to Lucy with the most revealing paragraph of all:

'What increased the value [of this information] was the speed with which the information reached us. One would normally think that a source producing information of such quality would take time to obtain it. No such delay occurred in the receipt of Lucy's information. On most occasions it was received within twenty-four hours of it being known at the appropriate headquarters in Berlin. *There was no question of any courier or safe hand-route. The information must have been received by Lucy over the air and his sources, whoever they were, must have gone almost hot-foot from the Service teleprinters to their wireless transmitters to send the information off'* (authors italics). There is only one catch; Rudolf Roessler—Lucy—neither possessed nor could he operate a radio transmitter.[2] And, even if he had been able to, the German *Abwehr* listening posts at Cranz and Stuttgart never again picked up an illegal radio transmitter *within* Germany after they had located the 'Red Orchestra's' transmitters, which were seized by the Gestapo in 1941–2.

Who then were Lucy's sources who went 'almost hotfoot from the Service teleprinters to their wireless transmitters'? There is only one answer to that question: a cunning, intricate, very devious one that must rank as one of Menzies' greatest triumphs in the Second World War: *The Secret Intelligence Service!*

When in early 1941 the 'Golf and Chess Club' at Bletchley first started breaking the intercepts which indicated that Germany was going to attack Russia, the news placed Menzies in a difficult situation. Like most of the old SIS hands he was a firm anti-communist; after all, his organization had spent most of its time in the late 'twenties and early 'thirties fighting the 'red danger'. But now Russia might soon be an ally and would need all the help she could get. What was he to do?

Winterbotham, who was still the head of the 'Shadow OKW', asked him what he should do with the information. C replied at once that naturally, 'We must let the PM have it.'

At that time Winterbotham was taking up to thirty messages a day to Churchill personally. 'But what about Stalin?' he asked.

'Yes, can we risk letting him know the source of information?' Menzies replied. 'We might well compromise the whole business.' The two men considered in silence for

---

[2] Rado also states that Lucy could not have been taught to use a transmitter by Taylor as has been sometimes stated. 'I know for sure,' he writes in his account of the network, 'that Schneider had no idea of radio technology and had never worked as an operator.'

a few moments, while the transcript of the vital message lay on the desk in front of them. Finally Winterbotham suggested: 'What about getting the PM to write a letter to Stalin, stating that it *looks* as if the Germans were going to attack Russia.'

Thus it was done, but not by letter. Churchill found the information of such tremendous importance that he instructed his Ambassador in Moscow, Sir Stafford Cripps, a left-winger himself, to advise Stalin *personally* of his assumptions based on 'sure information from a trusted agent'.

Cripps, of whom someone once said that he had 'lemonade instead of blood in his veins', was slow in getting to Stalin, but even when he did and predicted that the invasion would begin on 22 June, the exact day of Operation Barbarossa, Stalin refused to believe Churchill. 'Nothing that any of us could do,' Churchill wrote later, after paying glowing tribute to the 'agent', whom he never identified, 'pierced the purblind prejudice and fixed ideas that Stalin had raised between himself and the terrible truth.'[3]

Thus Menzies was prepared to go to the greatest lengths to protect the great Bletchley operation and learned in doing so just how suspicious the new Russian allies were of intelligence that did not come from their own sources.

Nor was Menzies prepared to disclose the source of his intelligence coups to the United States, not even to the man whom he had helped to become the first head of America's first intelligence organization, the OSS, the forerunner of the CIA.

Throughout the war Stephenson, the chief of the SIS in the Americas, made available to Donovan, head of the OSS, the deciphered wireless communications between Germany and the various *Abwehr* stations in South America. In fact the only information he was specifically barred from—on Menzies' order from London—was that dealing with enemy operations in the various war theatres. In particular, the Pacific and Far East. Why, I shall leave to the imagination of some anglophobe American historian or subscriber to the old theory of 'perfidious Albion'.

[3] Indeed Stalin, afraid of 'British provocations', went as far as ordering that agents who had predicted the German attack should be punished!

'On numerous occasions', Stephenson recalled after the war, 'when Donovan consulted me about reports and appreciations ... I would suggest alterations based upon the real rather than the deduced situations, as evidenced by these particular deciphered enemy communications ... I endeavoured to the end to get the Combined Chiefs of Staff to authorize *that Donovan should be made personally privy to this by far the most important source of secret intelligence, but it was never agreed.*' Even when the SIS learned in 1942 that an enemy agent had infiltrated the Czech Secret Service organization run by Colonel Pan in Lisbon—by the simple expedient of robbing the Czech diplomatic bag to the exiled government in London—they were unable to tell the Czech colonel that Bletchley had intercepted and decoded the enemy agent's signals to his chief in the Berlin headquarters of the *Abwehr*. For as the arch double-agent Kim Philby, who was in charge of operations in the Iberian Peninsula, expressed it: 'Our espionage abroad was primarily concerned with filling the gaps in the comprehensive picture (of the enemy) built up by the intercepts.'[4]

Back in 1941, however, when Menzies first started to get the details of the German plan to attack Russia, he must have puzzled how to transmit this information to the future ally without compromising his sources. The reaction to Churchill's approach through Sir Stafford Cripps soon showed him that the suspicious Russians would never accept such material at its face value; they would want to know more. As a result he would have to try a more sophisticated approach. And the best way to do that was to use the Soviets' own reserve espionage *Apparat* in Switzerland,[5] the presence of which was already known to him through the Czechs and probably the Swiss too, who knew that the only way to remove Germany's pressure from their own neutral island

[4] Pan proved impervious to the roundabout warning of the SIS. 'Tough as leather,' one agent described him. So the *Abwehr* spy within the Allied network continued to function and was indeed hired by the local OSS representative as a spy too in the end. Finally the only solution open to the SIS was to get rid of the OSS representative, which they did.
[5] The Dora ring did not become really operational until the invasion of Russia.

in the midst of a Nazi-occupied Europe was for the Germans to be so heavily engaged in Russia that they had no troops to spare to threaten 'poor little Switzerland'.[6]

It is very probable that it was Colonel Dansey, the deputy head of the SIS, who always guarded Switzerland as a base of operations with an almost proprietorial right, who ran the whole business. He had a key man in Switzerland, the last survivor of his pre-war Z organization van der Heuvel, who was supposedly a Count of the Holy Roman Empire; and it could well be that it was the Count who initiated the whole operation. Indeed what better place could there have been than neutral Switzerland for the great double-game? Diplomatic communications by both radio, located in Britain's various missions, and the diplomatic 'bag' were completely secure.

After November, 1942, when Lucy had sold himself to the Russians and the duped Director in Moscow was sending him congratulations and money bonuses, there was no longer any need for van der Heuvel. Foote could receive the key messages from London himself and pass them on, without Lucy's or Rado's knowledge. [The two naturally never met.]

Soon after this the character of his messages to the Russians began to change subtly. Prior to this time they had almost exclusively been concerned with military matters. Now Russia was winning and Menzies—and naturally Eden in the Foreign Office—wanted to convince the newly victorious Russians that Britain had no intention of making any serious overture to the Germans which could result in a separate peace. Nor did Eden, supported by Churchill, want the Russians to conquer territory which would make their presence a danger to British interests in the post-war world.

Thus we get 'urgent' messages from 'Olga' and 'Anna',[7] dated 25 April, 1943: 'The Germans believe that the Polish

[6] In this context it is interesting to note that as soon as it was clear that Russia was winning the war in the East, the Dora network was neatly rounded up by the Swiss; and that Rado was so compromised by his apparent attempt to contact the British that he was obviously heading for a labour camp if he ever returned to 'Mother Russia'.
[7] *Anna* being the German Foreign Office.

government in London assumes that the present war situation presents a greater danger for Poland than does the present German occupation.

'Hitler, Goering and Ribbentrop believe that this tactic can ... *poison English-Soviet relationships which can have an effect on the further course of the war.*' (author's italics)

One month later 'Olga' (The Luftwaffe HQ spy) informed the Director that 'Mannerheim[8] came to Switzerland to show officially to the Allies and Russia that Finland wanted to undertake no further obligations towards Germany in 1943'.

In that same month 'Werther' radioed the Director:

'The Bulgarian Czar Boris was forced to promise at his last meeting with Hitler that Bulgaria would join the war on the side of Germany and Rumania if there was any threat of an Anglo-Soviet occupation of the Dardanelles and the Bosphorus.'

Even the Pope was proved to be no threat to Russian interest, just as the Poles, Finns and Turks were not (according to the fake messages).

On 2 April, 1943, Foote radioed the Director:

'The Roman Pope and Cardinal Spellman spoke mainly about post-war politics ... According to the Pope, one can only seriously talk about a peace treaty and post-war possibilities after Hitler's fall, which will bring with it Mussolini's too.'

And so the great double game went on until the SIS found they no longer needed it, for by this time Menzies had already realized that Russia, now all-powerful and all-victorious, was going to replace Twelveland as the new enemy. Already he was toying with the idea of a new intelligence section, devoted to fighting Russia, the erstwhile ally, and considering whom he would appoint to lead it. In the end he decided on a bright new recruit to MI6, who had been brought into the organization by Vivian.

Thus as the Dora ring was wound up and Foote arrested— only after the Swiss police had conveniently left him enough time to destroy his codes, papers and radio—he named the new head of the anti-Soviet section—Philby.

[8] Head of the Finnish state and Germany's ally in the war against Russia.

Philby was to remark later that it was 'a piquant situation'. It was indeed.

In their evening chats just before Foote died, Muggeridge often attempted to draw him into discussing Lucy's sources and as Muggeridge wrote later, 'a knowing flicker of Foote's left eye left me no doubt that he for one, as an experienced radio operator, did not for one moment take seriously the possibility that Roessler received his information in a steady and undetected flow from the OKW.'

Just before Muggeridge met Foote for the last time, he attempted to find out from him what the real sources of Lucy's amazingly accurate messages were: did they really come, in fact, from Bletchley?

'I put the suggestion to Foote,' Muggeridge recalled.

Jim obviously did not like the question one bit. He 'looked faintly startled and then abruptly changed the subject'. And that was that; Muggeridge never did succeed in getting anything more out of him. Obviously the SIS had trained Foote well.

Yet, years later, when he recalled Bletchley Manor in the summer of 1941, with its croquet-playing dons, amateur violinists, chess-players—and cypher breakers, he wondered whether: '*if the Battle of Waterloo was won on the playing fields of Eton, the Battle of Stalingrad was, if not won, at any rate appreciably influenced on that remote lawn . . .*'

Book Two:

Triumph and Tragedy

'All that I can say is that I am a parson's son
and I was brought up as a Presbyterian, maybe
that makes me a fatalist, I don't know. But I
hope I have a reasonable moral standard.'
                              Allen Dulles, 1965.

PART ONE

THE YANKS ARE COMING

(1942–43)

'Overpaid, overfed, oversexed—and over here!'

British comment on the Americans, 1942

1

MR BULL ARRIVES IN BERNE

On 8 November, 1942, the day the Allies landed in North Africa, a tall American with greying hair and wire-rimmed glasses found himself trapped at Annemasse, the last railway station between Vichy-France and Switzerland.

The local Gestapo man had carefully noted the particulars in his passport and then ordered the French gendarme to inform him that these would have to be forwarded to Vichy itself for checking. With that he passed on to seek out other Anglo-Americans in this last train for Switzerland from Unoccupied France; for later that day German forces would march into Vichy France in answer to the threat posed by the Allied landing.

The American waited till he was out of earshot before taking his gendarme-guard to one side and making, as he recorded later, 'the most impassioned and, I believe, most eloquent speech that I had ever made in French. Evoking the shades of Lafayette and Pershing, I impressed upon him the importance of letting me pass. I had a valid passport and visa and there was no justification for holding me up.'

The American also let the French policeman have a glimpse at the contents of his wallet, which contained a large amount of what he was learning to call 'the slush fund'. But 'neither patriotic speeches nor the implied offer of a small fortune' seemed to move the Frenchman. A little later he moved off, leaving the American to worry about his fate.

Around noon, just about the time for the last train to leave for Switzerland, the gendarme returned and motioned the surprised traveller to board the train. '*Allez passez,*' he whispered, so no one could hear him. '*Vous voyez que notre collaboration n'est que symbolique'*. Apparently the Gestapo man had not allowed the North African landings and the impending German take-over of the Unoccupied Zone to interfere with his lunch.

The American needed no urging. He sprang into the train with surprising agility for a man who had sat behind a New York desk for so many years. Agent 110, code-named 'Mr Bull', the head of America's new intelligence organization, the OSS, had succeeded in getting into the heart of Hitler's *Festung Europa*. A few minutes later the last train crossed the Swiss Border on its way to Berne. After nearly two years of planning, the Office of Stategic Services was operational at last.

The concept of the OSS had been born in London in 1940, though no one recognized the fact at the time, for the man who gave birth to the idea was the failed saboteur, Stephenson.

When Stephenson fled back to London that summer he found that England's post-Dunkirk arsenals were empty and that the only place from which they could be replenished was the United States. But there was a difficulty—the sour-faced US Ambassador, Joseph Kennedy.

The Irish-American multi-millionaire was violently anti-British[1] and constantly informed his President that Britain was 'finished'. Even the advent of Winston Churchill made no difference to his attitude. It was, therefore, necessary to circumvent Kennedy if the British were to obtain the vitally needed arms from Roosevelt. Stephenson was given the task by Churchill of finding a powerful enough American, with the highest contacts possible, who might be able to get through to Roosevelt and plead Britain's cause. The man Stephenson found was Colonel William Donovan, a big, bluff Irish-American lawyer who was a member of the Republican Party but also an intimate of the Democratic President. Donovan, who possessed America's top three awards for valour, including the coveted Congressional

[1] Indeed it turned out that one of his aides, Tyler Kent, was a German spy at this time.

Medal of Honor won with the 'Fighting 69th' in the First World War, had long wished for a more exciting job and he jumped at the suggestion that he should tour Europe to report on Britain's capacity to fight. In the summer of 1940 he did exactly that, aided by the British, and returned to Washington where he speedily restored Roosevelt's confidence in Britain's fighting ability. As a result the supply of 'Lease Lend' goods started to flow across the Atlantic.

Five months later when Admiral Doenitz's submarines began to take a terrible toll of British convoys, Churchill ordered Stephenson, now installed as head of the SIS in the Americas in the Rockefeller Center, to use Donovan to persuade the US Navy to help convoy British ships across the Atlantic. Stephenson convinced Donovan he should report on the situation as the official representative of the US Navy. When Donovan agreed and was appointed, Stephenson radioed Menzies to let him have access to secret material too, stating: 'He can play a great role, perhaps a vital one, but it may not be consistent with orthodox diplomacy nor confined to its channels.'

One suspects that Menzies did not like this interference by his American station head in the top secret affairs of the SIS, for when Stephenson flew in with Donovan to London, it was the head of the SOE, Frank Nelson, who escorted him around the rival British spy organization's units scattered through the Home Counties, and not Menzies.

Thereafter Stephenson made sure that Donovan had a royal reception in the Mediterranean by getting Admiral Godfrey of Naval Intelligence to signal the Commander-in-Chief of the British Mediterranean Fleet a message, 'which made it abundantly clear to the Admiral and his staff that Donovan was the most important emissary that they were ever likely to meet in this world—or the next!'

Donovan returned to Washington feeling that 'he had never been treated in such an exalted fashion and that the red carpet had been thicker and wider than he thought it was possible to lay'. Donovan, the son of impoverished Irish emigrants to Buffalo, was sold on the aristocratic British leaders who ran the affairs of the embattled island. He reported to the President, who was so determined to tumble the great Empire those same leaders and their ancestors had built up, in glowing terms.

In 1941 the various secret departments of both the SOE and SIS began to supply Donovan with classified material which they hoped their 'advocate at court' would pass on to Roosevelt himself. In addition Stephenson urged Donovan to convince the President that the USA needed a secret intelligence organization of its own, for, Mussolini had joked the year before, 'the US Secret Service is the best in the world because no one knows where it is!' In other words, there wasn't one.

Although Churchill and his chief adviser on Intelligence, Major Desmond Morton, a great friend of Stephenson's, supported him, Menzies didn't like it. As Stephenson confessed later to Whitney Shepardson, one of Donovan's closest associates: 'Had it been comprehended in that building with which you are familiar [SIS Headquarters] to what extent I was supplying our friend with secret information to build up his candidacy for the position I wanted to see him achieve here, there would have been such a cold blast of horror sweep through it that on your first visit to it you would have had to find your way over one corpse after another!'

But Stephenson had his way. On 18 June, 1941, a reluctant Donovan was received by the President and convinced him to start an intelligence organization with himself as head Co-ordinator of Information (COI). Appointing him Major-General, Roosevelt confessed gloomily, 'You will have to begin with nothing. We have no intelligence service!'

Stephenson was jubilant in spite of the American lack of preparedness. He wired Menzies: 'You can imagine how relieved I am after three months of battle and jockeying for position in Washington that our man is in a position of such importance to our efforts!'

The SIS had created the first American intelligence organisation, the OSS, the forerunner of the CIA. They would live to rue that act of creation.

In the first months of America's new war, 'Hush-Hush Bill's' new spy organization was the joke of Washington's cocktail circuit. Its ranks full of college professors and New

Englanders with names straight out of the social register, its initials were said to mean 'Oh, So Silly', 'Oh, So Secret' or 'Organization Shush-Shush'.

Goebbels, speedily getting wind of its foundation, stated in a radio broadcast for the United States that it consisted of 'fifty professors, twenty monkeys, ten goats, twelve guinea pigs—and a staff of Jewish scribblers!'[2] And at first there was some justification for the mirth. With typical American 'get-up and go', the OSS new boys dreamed up a good number of crackpot schemes. There was the plan to load bats into a submarine and release them at dawn over the Japanese coast, where—to the terror of the Japanese—they would fly to the shade of a million homes, complete with a small incendiary bomb and time device! It was never carried out. But the one to flood the area of Berchtesgaden with pornography, which the experts calculated would unhinge Hitler's mind if he found it, was.[3] One wonders what the effect of that particular windfall was on the local Bavarian peasantry in the winter of 1943!

But slowly the crackpots and the fakes were weeded out of the organization and its first major batch of undertrained agents were sent to London under the command of an Ivy Leaguer, who one day would be the US Ambassador to that capital, Colonel David Bruce. The days of the cocktail circuit, the glamorous uniforms, the smart chatter were over; now the OSS would have to prove themselves under the critical eyes of the old hands, the Secret Intelligence Service.

One of the OSS men under the command of Colonel David Bruce was not quite so new at the game. He was Allen W. Dulles, a former partner in the New York legal firm of Sullivan and Cromwell, where up to quite recently many of his German business associates and clients had been the very men that Stephenson had so successfully compromised in the United States.[4]

---

[2] The strange reference to the animals is explained by the fact that Donovan had located some of his offices in the National Health Institute next to the experimental labs.

[3] The self-same experts were still peddling the same tired stories about Hitler's sex life—at the price of a dinner and drink—when I met them in Munich twenty years later.

[4] There was for instance, Kurt von Schroeder, who became an SS

In 1918, as a young member of the US Foreign Service, Dulles had been sent to Switzerland with a senior colleague, Hugh Wilson, to collect political information on Imperial Germany and the Austro-Hungarian Empire. There he had passed up an opportunity to meet a bearded young Russian revolutionary. His name was Lenin! Dulles swore he'd never disregard *any* source of information ever again. It was a resolution that would stand him in good stead in the years to come.

Thus, as Agent 110, code-named 'Mr Bull', finally reached Berne after crossing the Franco-Swiss frontier and settled into a new apartment in the Herrengasse, an arcaded and cobblestoned street running along the ridge high above the River Aare, he was returning to the scene of his apprenticeship. For 'Mr Bull' was Allen W. Dulles, OSS's chief-of-operations in Continental Europe.

general and who was a prime mover in channelling business funds from German industry into Himmler's coffers. Dulles had sat with him on the same board. Another associate of the international giant ITT—von Schroeder was on the board of one of its German companies—was Dr Gerhard Westrick, also an acquaintance of Dulles. Westrick, the elder brother of a member of Dr Adenauer's post-war German cabinet, was effectively forced out of the USA by Stephenson's disclosures, leaked to the *New York Herald-Tribune*.

During the course of Stephen's whispering campaign against the unfortunate Westrick the latter was besieged by a hostile group of New Yorkers whom he tried to appease by playing 'God Bless America' to them on his gramophone. They were 'not amused'. And he went.

2

HERRENGASSE 23

It was only a matter of weeks before the first of those Germans, hot-foot to betray their country, sneaked his way through the vineyards to meet the new master of Herrengasse 23. For Berlin had soon become aware of Dulles' presence in Berne and his true function. Even if the Germans had not broken his code, which they had, the international grapevine had already spread the word that Dulles was all right—conservative, not virulently anti-German, a friend of big business and, if we are to believe later SD reports, anti-Jewish. And, as had been the case with the contacts made by the SIS three years before, the first 'resister' was associated with both Canaris's *Abwehr* and Ribbentrop's Foreign Office.

He was Dr Hans Bernd Gisevius, a Prussian lawyer who, after being dismissed from the Gestapo, the Police and almost from the *Abwehr* too, was now stationed in Switzerland under the cover of vice-consul, where he continued to carry out his intelligence work.

The SIS, with whom Gisevius had had dealings back in 1939, did not trust him; they thought him opportunistic and self-seeking. For his part Gisevius had gone sour on the SIS too. 'There had been only occasional meetings,' he wrote after the war, 'because the Allies (the French were involved too) restricted themselves largely to pure espionage. The British, above all, stuck to the old-fashioned scheme in which the "enemy" was considered solely as an object of espionage.'

Gisevius, however, was not content to be only a spy. He aimed at a political role and he felt he had found in Dulles a spymaster, who would allow him to do just that. 'Dulles,' he recalled, 'was the first intelligence officer who had the courage to extend his activities to the political aspects of the war ... Everyone breathed easier; at last a man had been found with whom it was possible to discuss the contradictory complex of problems emerging from Hitler's war!'

In spite of the fact that Edge Leslie of the Swiss SIS station warned Dulles against Gisevius, Dulles persisted and nearly came to grief right at the start.

One evening, when Gisevius was dining with Dulles, the latter's German-speaking cook, eavesdropping at the door, was struck by the un-Swiss character of his visitor's German.[1]

Quietly she tip-toed away and picked up Gisevius's hat to examine it. It was, as she had suspected, of German manufacture. Swiftly, like the trained agent she was, she scribbled down the initials of its owner in the sweat-band and disappeared back into her kitchen.

The next morning, while out shopping for Dulles's dinner, she slipped into the German legation and reported her findings to her contact there. It did not take him long to identify the owner of the hat with the initials 'HBG'.

But Gisevius had been a conspirator now for nearly a decade. He easily outbluffed his accusers, maintaining that he had met Dulles on a special mission for Admiral Canaris. He swore his accusers to secrecy and admonished them never to mention the matter again. It is recorded that they even apologized to him.

Gisevius was the first of a flood of high-placed, right-wing Germans who came to visit number 23 Herrengasse, bearing their snippets of 'hard' intelligence, plus their 'proposals for a new Germany'. They included former Rhodes scholar and now Foreign Office official Adam von Trott zu Solz who, while busily engaged plotting a revolution in Germany against Hitler, was also a moving force in the plan to sweep the British out of India with the aid of the Indian nationalist Chandra Bose; *Abwehr* men, Eduard Waetjen, like Gisevius a lawyer, and Theodor Struenck, a director of a large Frankfurt insurance firm; Otto Karl Kiep, who represented the

---

[1] There is a great and easily recognizable difference between Swiss-German and that spoken by native Germans.

German Foreign Office in the *Abwehr*; Ambassador Friedrich Werner; Count von der Schulenburg, who had been Hitler's envoy in Moscow at the time of the notorious Stalin-Hitler non-aggression pact. And there were the businessmen too, eager to be on the winning side, confident of being received by Dulles in the manner befitting their status, for, after all, he was one of them: a representative of 'big business'.[2]

But those right-wing intriguers and their 'big business' allies would have been surprised to learn that the master of 23 Herrengasse had also made contact with the survivors of the communist 'red orchestra' network in Germany through the agency of Noel Field, whose father had been one of his most valuable contacts during the time he had spent in Switzerland in the First World War.

Field had been accused of being a communist agent while working for the State Department but he had wriggled out of the charge, had resigned and joined the League of Nations staff in Geneva. In 1941 he had been appointed director of the Unitarian Service Committee in Unoccupied France and, like Dulles, had managed to slip into Switzerland before the border had closed. There he had continued his work of aiding refugees from fascism, a valuable cover for his work with the communists. He, also, began to help Dulles unofficially.

Dulles, who knew of his communist sympathies, called him a 'romantic idealist'. A young OSS officer who knew him at that time and was to make a name for himself in later years, Arthur Schlesinger Jr, was more forthright. 'What struck me most was his self-righteous stupidity. He was a Quaker Communist, filled with smugness and sacrifice and not a very intelligent man.' All the same, Field managed to link Dulles up with what was left of the German communist network, which had been built up from Sweden by the ex-communist *Reichstag* deputy Herbert Wehner and his long-time associate Leo Bauer. Although both men went to jail

---

[2] Some of these German emissaries to Dulles did pay, however, the supreme penalty for what—from the German point-of-view—was treachery. Trott zu Solz, Kiep and Struenck were all executed after the abortive 1944 attempt on Hitler's life.

for spying in late 1942, Noel Field kept Dulles' communist contacts going and they were to prove useful in the last months of the war, as we shall see.[3]

But in late 1942 and early 1943 all Dulles's contacts, right-wingers as well as left-wingers, who had bungled along for years without even seriously coming close to achieving their aim of getting rid of Hitler, were amateurs. And as amateurs they were duly laughed at by the professionals in the Broadway Headquarters of the SIS. After all Bletchley could read both the German *Abwehr* and Foreign Office messages; what information of any importance could this lawyer-turned-spymaster in Berne supply them with which they didn't know about already?

In the spring of 1943, however, all that changed. For now Menzies realized that the Americans were trying to sneak into the first league. Dulles had been approached by the real professionals, Schellenberg's SD. It was time that the SIS took a hand in the affairs of Allen W. Dulles.

As far back as August, 1942, when there was still every possibility that Germany might win the war, Schellenberg, who would have been a man after Menzies' heart,[4] surprised his chief with the question: 'Reichsführer, in what drawer of your desk do you keep an alternative solution for ending the war?'

Himmler, who was now proud of the fact that he was

[3] All three men made amazing post-war careers. Wehner changed his allegiance to the German socialist party and returned to West Germany—some say with the aid of the SIS—to become Willy Brandt's right-hand man, the SPD party ideologist, and present head of the SPD's parliamentary faction. Leo Bauer, after being dismissed from his important post in the communist East German régime and sentenced to twenty-five years' imprisonment as a 'Western spy', went west in 1952 to become Willy Brandt's chief political adviser. He died recently. Noel Field, however, caused the biggest sensation of all when he and virtually his whole family disappeared behind the Iron Curtain in 1949.

[4] Like young men will he indulged himself; for instance in a bullet-proof desk, with built-in twin machine guns which he could fire from his chair in case of attack by one of his visitors. But apart from such little weaknesses he was a cynical, realistic office-seeker. It is, therefore, not surprising that Menzies saved him from the gallows after the war and ensured that he only received a light sentence at Nuremburg, since he was clearly a man who would be ready to serve a new master.

'the most feared man in Europe', flushed angrily: 'Have you gone crazy?' he demanded.

But Schellenberg, who Himmler thought had saved his life (he had dragged him away from an open door in an aeroplane) soon calmed the Reichsführer. In his glib way, he explained that there must be some means of ending the war in the West while continuing the fight against the 'red hordes' in the East.

Himmler bought the idea. Somewhat hesitantly 'loyal Heinrich', as Hitler was wont to call him, gave Schellenberg permission to make contact with Allied representatives in a neutral country.

The man Schellenberg picked to make his contact was one of his most influential agents, Prince Max Egon von Hohenlohe-Langenburg-Rothenhaus, who lived in Spain. Although Stalingrad was not yet lost, Schellenberg told the Prince (according to his own statement) that 'the West would not sign a peace with Hitler; therefore political changes would have to take place within Germany. He hoped that Hitler would be patriotic enough to resign in the interest of the German People. If he didn't, however, *violence could not be ruled out!*'

The unthinkable idea had been born.

Hohenlohe had his first talks with the Americans in Lisbon, but in January, 1943, he changed his rendezvous to Berne and his American contact to Allen Dulles, whom he had known in the First World War. Dulles reinforced von Hohenlohe's old opinion of him. According to the report he sent to Schellenberg, '[he was] fed up with listening all the time to outdated politicians, émigrés and prejudiced Jews!' The American believed (again according to the SD report, which was revealed to the press much later when Dulles was the head of the CIA)[5] that Germany would play an important role in the postwar world as 'a factor of order and progress' and the base of a 'cordon sanitaire against Bolshevism'. Purportedly larding his statement with

[5] By the Russians naturally. Even so it is terribly hard to find out the true details of those meetings, indeed of all the meetings in the *Herrengasse*; for seemingly they could implicate too many powerful people in both West Germany and the USA.

anti-semitic and anti-British sentiments, Dulles said he did not 'reject National Socialism in its basic ideas and deeds'. However he did warn that the Americans would never accept Hitler as the 'unchallenged master of Greater Germany'.

The idea began to ripen.

At a meeting with von Hohenlohe on 21 March, 1943, Dulles's colleague Roberts was more explicit. For his part he couldn't 'see how Hitler, whose signature had lost all credit, could be accepted by the Allies'.

Schellenberg took the hint. Hitler would have to be removed before the American government would deal with the Reichsführer.

The plan to assassinate Hitler nearly came to grief at the start. Himmler sent an old acquaintance, a lawyer named Carl Langbehn, to Switzerland to sound out the British Ambassador on his reaction to the plan. It was decided that a member of the British Embassy should fly to London with his recommendation and put it before the government. Accordingly London was informed by radio.

Thus it was that the Embassy, under whose auspices the great Foote double operation was carried out, allowed the message to be sent to London in a code that they knew from their own Bletchley operation the Germans could crack.

The Germans duly did. In September the deciphered message, which had been broken by the General Staff's decoding section in Berlin, was passed on to Hitler. The Führer summoned Himmler, who just managed to talk himself out of the situation. But as a result of that meeting, Langbehn was sent to a concentration camp and a shaken Himmler told Schellenberg, 'It was just pure chance that the whole business did not have the most unpleasant consequences for me.'

But Schellenberg was not prepared to abandon his plan. He dreamed up 'Operation KN'. 'KN' for kidnapping. This time he avoided Switzerland and made contact with the Americans through the German police attaché at the German embassy in Madrid, Paul Winzer. Winzer, who had built up a network of agents throughout Spain, which were supervised by a French *émigré* named Letellier, was ordered to prepare to help the plotters to kidnap the Führer.

But, before the plan could be executed, Letellier broke into Winzer's safe and sold the KN Plan papers to a member of the SIS.

Who that member of the SIS was we shall learn in due course; but when the news of the failure of Schellenberg's plan reached Dulles he was not unduly worried. He knew that the group of plotters with whom Gisevius was associated were still planning Hitler's assassination, even if Schellenberg had given up for the time being. Besides he had just contacted the 'intelligence officer's dream', the man who was 'not only our best source on Germany, but undoubtedly one of the best secret agents any intelligence service has ever had'. George Wood, America's number one spy in Twelveland throughout the Second World War, had arrived on the scene.

3

ALIAS GEORGE WOOD

On the morning of 23 August, 1943, Gerald Meyer, one of Dulles's assistants, who had been born in Frankfurt and spoke German fluently, was working his way through the usual pile of morning mail when his secretary came in to announce that a 'Dr Brown' would like to see him.

Meyer told his secretary to send the man in. He turned out to be a German who had a vague contact with a banker whom Meyer had met briefly a few months before in Basel. While Meyer listened, bored and not a little cynical—Switzerland was full of types like this trying to get off the hook before it was too late—'Dr Brown' went into a long and complicated explanation for his being there. After a while Meyer grew impatient and asked him to come to the point. Whereupon 'Dr Brown' reached into the pocket of his suit and pulled out a large envelope from which he extracted three sheets. Each was addressed to the German Foreign Minister, signed by an important official in Ribbentrop's Ministry—Abetz, von Papen, von Neurath—and bore the magic legend '*geheime Reichssache*'.[1]

The young OSS aide asked his visitor where he had obtained such important documents. 'Dr Brown' turned cagey. 'I am merely acting as an emissary for a friend who works in the Foreign Office,' he said. 'This man is now in Berne. He arrived yesterday as a special diplomatic courier, which is only a cover for his real purpose. In reality he has come here in order to make contact with the Allies.'

Meyer excused himself and went upstairs to Dulles's office. He put the documents on his boss's desk and gave him a quick explanation. Dulles sat back. 'There are three

[1] State Secret.

122

possibilities,' he said. 'This could be an attempt to break our code.[2] The Germans figure we'll bite, cipher this stuff and radio it on to Washington. They monitor everything, including the Swiss commercial radio channels. They'll be listening for these dispatches in the hope that a foreknowledge of the contents will give them the clue they need to decipher it. Or perhaps our friend is an *agent provocateur*. He plants information with us and then tips off the Swiss police that we are spying. His rendezvous with us is proof and we are kicked out of the country. Still,' he concluded, 'there is just the glimmer of a chance that this man is on the square.'

Thus it was decided that 'Dr Brown' should be informed that Meyer was prepared to meet him and his source in his own apartment—at midnight. It was all in the best Hollywood spy thriller tradition.

That evening the German visitor turned up promptly at midnight, following 'Dr Brown' into the room. He was a small balding man in his early forties, dressed in a dark leather jacket. Meyer offered to take his coat and the man nodded but before he did so, he dug his right hand into the pocket and drew out a large brown envelope, a swastika stamp on its red wax seal.

Without any preamble he said in a Berlin accent, 'Dr Brown has already told you that I have more material for you. If my memory serves me right, there are one hundred and eighty-six separate items of information in this.' He tossed the envelope on the table.

Hurriedly Meyer leafed through them. Most of them looked as if they were copies of telegrams sent by German Foreign Office officials overseas—morale of the troops in Russia, details of sabotage in France, notes on the visit of the Japanese ambassador etc. As he examined them, Dulles walked in, as agreed, and was introduced as Mr Douglas.

'You gentlemen will ask whether these dispatches are authentic and if so how I was able to get them,' the German said. 'They came from the material which crossed my own

[2] Dulles need not have worried; the Germans had already broken his code. Just like the SIS, the *Abwehr* and the SD were monitoring his transmissions to the States.

123

desk in the Foreign Office.' He went on to say that he was chief assistant to Dr Karl Ritter, the Foreign Office liaison officer to the *Wehrmacht*, to whom a mass of information flowed from the German missions abroad.

Dulles and Meyer changed glances. They knew Karl Ritter. He was a notorious pre-war spy, whose last mission in South America had ended in scandal. But they did not say anything and their visitor continued. He had been a member of the Foreign Office since 1925, had risen to first secretary and was a convinced nationalist, but he was still opposed to the Nazis. For years he had bottled up his opposition, but now he was in a position to do something in the 'fight against the Nazis'.

Week after week he had made surreptitious copies of the top secret documents which crossed his desk in Berlin, waiting for an opportunity like this. 'From the very first day that I had dealings with secret documents, it was clear to me that I would have to find a way to get them out,' he said. 'Even before Pearl Harbor I made an attempt to contact the Americans through the Church, but it didn't work out.'

Then he had thought of his many friends in Switzerland and had decided that he must find a way of contacting them. Telling the authorities that he had to have a visa in order to go to Switzerland to divorce his second wife who was Swiss, he had tried to get out that way but failed. Then luck played into his hands and he was selected to go to Switzerland as an official courier.

'What are your conditions [for working for us],' Dulles asked.

'Gentlemen' he said, 'I hate the Nazis. For me they are the arch-enemy. I feel the same about the communists. Both are a threat for the world. But we're in the middle of a war and there is no time for bargaining. Please try to believe that I am a patriotic German. All I need for my services is help, encouragement and support after the war.'

'It's hard to say what will happen after the war,' Dulles replied. 'It's got to be won first.' He touched the wooden table-top for luck.

It was now three o'clock in the morning. But before the

unexpected agent left, Dulles decided to give him a name; it was Wood, George Wood.

Wood, whose real name was Fritz Kolbe,[3] had not been entirely honest with his new boss that night. For he had already approached another allied intelligence organization the day before—the SIS. And their representatives had thrown him out on his ear. Kolbe was virulently anti-communist so he could not approach the Soviet Secret Service (as we shall soon see, they learned of his approach to the Americans without much delay) and all that was left to him was Mr Bull.

And Mr Bull was overjoyed with the contents of that first envelope. After staying up the whole night to examine them, he radioed Washington and asked for permission to employ Wood, forwarding the information he had brought with him for examination by the diplomatic pouch. But already Wood had run into trouble.

Hardly had he arrived back in his Berlin office when he was summoned to the local security officer. 'You were the courier to Berne?' he asked.

'Yes.'

'It has come to our attention that you spent most of the night of 23rd/24th *not* in your bed in the Hotel Terminus.'

'That's right,' Wood answered, smiling coldly. Sometimes one needs a bit of a change—a couple of drinks, a girl.'

'Very frivolous,' his interlocutor snapped.

'I agree,' Wood said and pulled out a doctor's *Attest.* 'That's why I took certain precautions.'

The security officer looked at the doctor's note which certified that Wood had received a prophylactic injection and a blood test on the morning of 24 August, 1943, 'All right,' he said. 'But take better care how you spend your time in the future.' Wood would live to spy on.

In the next weeks Wood worked like mad to obtain

[3] Although my request for information to the present German Foreign Office was kindly supported by a German cabinet minister, its officials were not eager to disclose more than the barest information about Dulles' number one spy. They limited themselves to details which could be confined to one sentence.

fresh information for Dulles in Berne. It is hard to explain, at this distance of time, why he took such great risks and worked at such a tremendous rate. Can one explain it by his former allegiance to the socialist party and consequent hatred of the Nazis? Did his failure to obtain real promotion in the Foreign Office after nearly twenty years of service play a role? Or did his two broken marriages and lack of a settled home-life trigger off the decision to betray his own country on such a tremendous scale? (Before he had finished, he had passed on 27,000 separate items of intelligence to Dulles.)

We know little of his reasons, but we do know that during that summer of 1943 he collected a tremendous amount of material, including a detailed account of Japanese naval and military strength and dispositions, plus information about the reinforcement of the German Italian front facing the US Fifth Army. Sometimes he left his office in the evening, with copied secret material filling his pockets to overflowing.

By the end of October he had decided it was time to go to Berne again. In addition to the material already collected, he had discovered that the German Embassy in Dublin had set up a secret transmitter to direct U-boat attacks on the Atlantic convoys. Wood had also come to the conclusion that a telegram from Germany's Madrid mission reading 'Ships with cargoes of oranges will continue to sail' meant that Franco had broken an agreement with the Allies not to supply Germany any longer with Tungsten. And he was in luck. He was ordered to travel to Berne as a German Foreign Office courier once again.

But this time Wood knew that the journey would not be so easy. Although it normally took eighteen hours from Berlin, Allied air raids could make a two day affair out of it; and every minute that he was in Germany with the incriminating material on his person would be sheer torture.

Accordingly he made his precautions. Instead of tying the secret material to his leg as he had done the first time, he smuggled it inside the official material he was carrying and had it sealed with the red swastika. Before the train carrying him to Switzerland left the Anhalter Bahnhof he gave the guard a large tip and told him he would like to be wakened first if there were an Allied air attack. He explained to the guard that he was of a nervous disposition and it would be a great comfort to him if he knew that the guard would rouse him in an emergency. In reality, Wood wanted to have time to destroy his secret material if the situation grew critical.

At four o'clock that morning, the guard knocked at the door of his compartment and bellowed '*Fliegeralarm*'. Wood woke with a start. The train had already stopped. The air attack was imminent. Grabbing his case, Wood dropped to the ground and hid in a ditch as the noise of the Allied bombers grew louder and louder.

Wood cowered in the ditch as the raid passed. The bombers missed the train but they hit the line ahead and when dawn came Wood saw the huge hole in the track. A nightmare of a day followed before a relief train came to collect them and they could continue their journey. Wood was a bundle of nerves when he reached the border, but he passed through the German checks at the Badische Bahnhof, in the German sector of Basel, without any difficulty. Taking a taxi across the Rhine bridge to the Swiss station there, he removed the secret material from its hiding place in one of the toilets and took the next train to Berne. After delivering the German dispatches to his own legation he contacted Dr Brown.

Brown told him that the Americans had been waiting for him for weeks; he was to meet Meyer, who would be driving an English Triumph at the Kirchenfeld Bridge. Again the time would be midnight. The OSS were carrying out their clandestine rendezvous in the strict tradition of the classic spy novel.

The Germans had forced a blackout on the Swiss—they maintained the British were using the Swiss lights as a guidelight, which indeed they were—and thus Wood waited alone on the bridge until a single blue light flashing on and off twice indicated that Meyer was coming. Seconds later he drove up in his little British sports car. Wood got in and was whisked off to the Herrengasse. Over a glass of good Scotch to calm his nerves, he told Dulles all he knew—the

German plan to force the Vichy French to shoot any member of De Gaulle's forces captured as traitors; the German legation in Buenos Aires had signalled that a large Allied convoy had left for Britain, etc, etc, etc.

Wood told him that he had worked out a complicated code through which to communicate with Dr Brown. He also suggested a way in which they could tell him that they had received the information. 'Dr Brown can get someone to send me food parcels—sardines, butter, coffee and the like. But they must be sent regularly. When you have received information from me, you put coffee in the parcel, but then only. I shall know if I receive coffee that everything has gone off all right.'

Thus in the somewhat mundane manner, which at least ensured that Wood received a consignment of precious *Bohnenkaffee*, worth a fortune on the German black market, the problem of transmitting secret material was solved.

Just before he left Wood asked for two favours. The first was a camera. 'If I can photograph the material it will save me a lot of time.'

Meyer agreed to supply him with one the next day.

The next request was for a revolver. It was a request which Meyer refused. It would be too risky to be found with one in his possession if he were arrested.

Wood shrugged and gave a faint smile. As they shook hands in parting, he said. 'It doesn't matter. I'll get one in Germany, I don't intend to liquidate the *Wehrmacht* with it. I shall only use it in the greatest emergency—*for myself*!'

And with that he was gone.[4]

---

[4] Wood continued to spy for the OSS right to the end, using other Germans as couriers between Berlin and Berne in addition to the encoded messages. Dulles saw him only once more, at the beginning of 1944. He had learned of the attempt to kill Hitler and he told Dulles he wanted to give up his spying and join the plotters. He was scared that any new German government would stamp him as a spy. If he were a member of the opposition, it would enable him to achieve some sort of position in the 'new Germany'. Dulles, who already knew the plotters had been infiltrated by the SD, convinced him he should continue to work as a spy. Thus George Wood, America's master spy, carried out his spying right to the end to disappear then into obscurity. If he's alive today, he would be seventy-three.

4

THE OLD FIRM TAKES A HAND

Wood's material was greeted in the United States with tremendous enthusiasm. Even President Roosevelt, who was no friend of espionage, asked to see it. Stephenson was equally enthusiastic about it. He wrote to Donovan much later, after Dulles had visited him from Switzerland: 'The visit here of your very able representative in Switzerland reminds me of the fact that when I was in London recently, I had an opportunity of going into the history and product of the 'Wood' traffic. This is certainly one of the greatest secret intelligence achievements of this war.'[1]

But back at the SIS headquarters there were those who were decidedly not of the same opinion—Colonel Claude Dansey, in particular. Loyally enough Dulles had the first batch of Wood's material copied and sent to London, where Dansey, now heavily engaged in the Lucy operation and some mysterious work with the film producer Alexander Korda and the Jewish League (it was to earn both of them a knighthood), was enraged by Dulles's activity in his pet Swiss reserve. He gave the material a quick examination and pronounced the Wood documents a fake and a German 'plant'. Felix Cowgill, head of the SIS's counter-intelligence section, agreed. Though originally a Vivian man, Cowgill had realized that Dansey had C's ear and had hitched his star to Dansey.

Thus, in the autumn of 1943 when Cowgill had to fly

[1] This letter, with its expression of 'my sincere admiration for the way your whole S.I. organization has been developed' incidentally encouraged Donovan to propose, *three days later*, to President Roosevelt that the USA should set up a permanent post-war secret intelligence organization. It was the first reference to the organization which later became the CIA.

across the Atlantic to confer with his OSS counterparts in Washington, he felt he had to order one of his subordinates to examine the Wood documents more carefully and 'prove' that they were a fake. In this manner he would gain, he assumed, Dansey's favour. That subordinate was a relatively new recruit to his Section V; his name was Kim Philby.

Since the discovery of the full extent of Kim Philby's treachery was made in the early '60s, much has been made of his background, giving the impression he was some sort of upper class charmer, who got into the SIS through the old-boy network, 'complaisant passenger in a racketeering upper class world'.

But, apart from his education, his background was anything but upper class. His grandmother was Anglo-Indian, with all that that implies. His father was an opinionated office-seeker who finally found a financial and sexual niche toadying to Middle Eastern princes. His cronies, his drinking habits and the squalor of his affairs and marriages were in no way consistent with 'breeding'. And there was that appalling stutter, which totally muffled any 'upper class' accent he might have had. As Muggeridge, who knew him well, recalled, 'He might have been speaking broad cockney, Glaswegian—Scottish or stage Yorkshire, but no one would ever have known, so strangled and malformed were the words that finally emerged from his tormented mouth.'

With the exception of 'C' himself, his colleagues on the SIS permanent staff were not upper class. They were routine office-seekers, like himself, who were always consciously fighting for position and advancement. And it was because he recognized this fact early in his SIS career that he made such a success of it. Thus, when Cowgill went to America and left him with the Wood papers, Philby saw that his chance had come. For him 'Cowgill, Vivian, Dansey, the Chief . . . were all parts of a jigsaw puzzle' and it was difficult for him from his lowly position to guess how they might react when he confronted them with his findings. At all events he decided that he had to make a thorough and objective examination of the Wood documents so that there would be no chance of a slip-up.

And then he had a brilliant idea. Most of the documents

seemed to him to be German Foreign Office telegrams. Could it be that Denniston might have already deciphered the same telegrams and that he, Philby, might be able to compare Wood's documents with the intercepts? Checking through them again, he found a note from Dansey empowering Cowgill to do 'what you think necessary'. Covered by this, he contacted Denniston.

By 1942 Denniston, aided by Dilly Knox, had achieved notable success. As we have already seen, Bletchley had informed Churchill of the German halt outside Dunkirk, the end of the plan to invade England. (Incidentally Churchill kept this information top secret in order to gain Roosevelt's support and sympathy for the 'threatened island' which was already saved from invasion) and had helped to sink the Bismarck.[2] In that same year Bletchley also delivered the full plan of the German invasion of Crete from the air, although little use was apparently made of it. One year later Montgomery was presented with the full order-of-battle and plans of Rommel's *Afrika Korps* just before El Alamein. Indeed if the full history of that operation in Hut Three at Bletchley were known, it would undoubtedly mean a rewriting of much of the history of the Second World War.

But Denniston's very success had gained him powerful enemies, in particular Menzies. And Denniston was in many ways his own worst enemy. He was impatient, secretive and quarrelsome. He fell out not only with Whitehall but also with his own colleagues, who were irritated by his elaborate screen of secrecy. Thus, after he fell ill in 1942, when he recovered Menzies had him transferred to a small office in London where his job was to break German Foreign Office messages. His place at Bletchley was taken by Commander Edward Travis, who later received a knighthood about which all the old SIS hands seem to talk continually. And so it was at his new office that Philby contacted Denniston.

Denniston, always eager to check the accuracy of his own operation, was glad to compare his results with the telegrams that Philby sent him. Three days later he telephoned Philby

---

[2] It is reliably reported that Bletchley knew the ship's position the whole time. Reconnaissance planes were sent out to 'look for it' in order to fool the Germans that the British had not broken the navy codes.

to inform him that he had already cracked the same tele-grams—and could Philby send more.

Philby could. In the next days he sent as many as Dennis-ton could manage. Then, after Denniston had shown that one third of the Wood material was genuine, Philby took his plot a step further. He began sending the Wood material to the service intelligence organizations. They clamoured for more. After a while Philby asked them and Denniston for letters certifying to the letters' usefulness and accuracy. They obliged and now Philby knew it was time to go and beard Colonel Dansey.

His interview with Dansey was a very unpleasant half-hour. The Deputy Head of the SIS was beside himself with rage after Philby had stuttered out an explanation of what he had done. Didn't he, Philby, know that this would en-courage the OSS people to go stamping around all over Switzerland spreading their absurd network? Why, in a matter of days they could endanger his own carefully built-up spy-ring. (He referred to the Lucy group.)

Philby let him finish before pointing out that the other service intelligence departments did not know this was OSS material. They thought it came from the SIS. It was a telling point. It would do him no harm if the military intelligence department felt indebted to him for this material. In the end he dismissed Philby, saying, 'Carry on then. You're not such a fool as I thought you were!'

The Wood business was a minor triumph for Philby and another step on the road to the position he coveted. Dansey, the most feared man in the SIS, had been bearded in his den and he had come out of the confrontation unharmed; indeed his reputation had been increased.

Dansey had recognized a fellow spirit, admittedly a new boy and a university graduate, but one who knew how to use the corridors of power to his own advantage.

Soon Philby was to get rid of his chief, Felix Cowgill, by making Vivian doubt his loyalty and become the first head of Section 9, the anti-Soviet intelligence group which was set up *before* the Western Allies had landed in Normandy in 1944.

But that was the future. In mid-1943 Philby contented

himself with using his newly established position to run the Iberian operations of Section V without any real control. Bribery, burglary, blackmail—and, if we are to believe John le Carré, perhaps even political murder[3]—were all part and parcel of his daily work. Who engineered the theft of Schellenberg's Plan KN from the police attaché's safe in Madrid? Philby. When an SIS analyst, probably Hugh Trevor-Roper, wrote a paper arguing that there was a serious split in Germany between the Party and the High Command and that the *Abwehr* might well make further approaches to the SIS with real peace feelers, Philby blocked the paper resolutely and without any explanation (but he could not prevent General Donovan meeting Admiral Canaris somewhere in Spain in that same year).

Thus while the new boy Dulles blundered his way through the confused Central European jungle of espionage, double-dealing and deceit and Wood sweated out his furtive existence in Berlin, both believing they were obtaining important new material, although it had long been known in Bletchley and London, Philby used them to further his own interests. But if Dulles' 'intelligence officer's dream' was of little real value, one tiny item from 'Mr Bull' was of such importance that it occupied the attention of the SIS's most unusual operative for most of that summer—even after it had turned out to be false.

[3] In the introduction to *Philby: The Spy Who Betrayed a Generation* (Page, Leitch and Knightly) Mr le Carré writes: 'For those who enjoy tortuous speculation there is one intriguing coincidence. Sikorski, whose assassination Rolf Hochhuth notoriously attributes to Winston Churchill, took off from Gibraltar on 4 July, 1943. At that time Kim Philby was in charge of SIS counter-intelligence operations in the Iberian Peninsula. If Sikorski *was* assassinated, is it conceivable that Philby planned the operation on behalf of his Russian masters, and that the assassin whom he hired believed he was working for the British?'

PART TWO

THE PEENEMUENDE PLAN

(1943–44)

'The following specific targets of the enemy's Intelligence network have come to the attention of the High Command's military Intelligence service: what is our present tank output; what is our present aircraft output; *what kind of new weapons does Germany plan to use in the coming total warfare?*'

Abwehr *Circular to Wehrmacht Military Districts, 1943.*

1

SIS PLAYS THE JOKER

In early 1943, Dr Stanley P. Lovell, a middle-aged scientist whom Donovan called his 'Professor Moriarty' and who was in charge of the OSS's 'Department of Dirty Tricks', was leafing his way through a pile of carbons of the OSS messages covering the last twenty-four hours when he came across one which read: 'One of my men got dry clothes and a breakfast for a French *ouvrier* who swam the Rhine to Rehen last night. Told following improbable story. Said he was forced labor guard for casks of water from Rjukan in Norway to island of Peenemuende in Baltic Sea.'

Dr Lovell put the message into his out-tray, then changed his mind and took it out; a week earlier he had attended a discussion by scientists involved in top-secret nuclear fission studies at which someone had remarked: 'I think graphite would be a more efficient neutron arrester than heavy water.' Now an unknown French worker turns up in Switzerland, maintaining he had been forced to guard water—the only water in the world worth guarding was Deuterium or heavy water.

Lovell called for maps of Europe and the OSS encyclopaedias. Rjukan turned out to be the biggest hydro-electric development in Europe and the most probable location in the continent where 'heavy water' might be produced. Lovell then called for the USAF photos of Usedom, the peninsula on the Baltic on the landward tip of which Peenemuende was located. He could see nothing. 'Dairy farms, thatched farmhouses—a peaceful, bucolic spectacle if I ever saw one,' he recalled later.

All the same he went straight away to see General Donovan. 'Bill,' he said, 'this may be vitally important.'

Donovan asked Lovell to explain. Lovell told Donovan of the great Manhattan Project, later to build the world's first atomic bomb. 'This little French workman,' he said, 'has told us where the German heavy water comes from, but vastly more important, where the German physicists are working to make a bomb employing nuclear fission. It all adds up perfectly.'

'Adds up to what?'

'To a catastrophic Nazi victory. This explains the ski sites.'

Lovell showed him a secret map of the French 'ski' sites, so named because from the air they looked like a forty-foot ski laid on edge. He explained that there were presently seventy-odd such structures from Hazebrouck, west of Boulogne, to Valognes, south of Cherbourg.

'Remember what Hitler said,' Lovell went on, ' "We will have a weapon to which there is no answer"? The whole thing falls into place. Every ski site is pointed directly at London, Bristol, Birmingham and Liverpool. They must be launching sites for unmanned missiles containing enough nuclear fission bombs to destroy each of those cities utterly. Britain can't resist if they're obliterated. If we bomb the very hell out of Peenemuende we stop it cold before it has a chance to start.'

Thus it was that Dr Lovell found himself on a plane to tell his story to Colonel Bruce in London. At once Bruce contacted Lord Portal of the RAF and General Spaatz of the 8th Air Force in Britain. Thereafter, according to Lovell, 'by persuasion and . . . diplomacy . . . we got the Peenemuende air raid laid on and delayed the use of the V-1s and V-2s until after the Normandy landings in June, 1944.'

Dr Lovell was mistaken about the result of his visit to London. The RAF did not bomb Peenemuende in August, 1943, because of his report; by the time he arrived in England they had already known about the German research centre for nearly six months and his information about the heavy water was incomplete (actually it was not sent to Peenemuende from Rjukan but to the *Kaiser Wilhelm Institut*). But his information did serve as another stimulus to the strange scientist who had been directing the SIS's scientific air intelligence against Twelveland since 1939, Dr R. V. Jones.

Reginald Jones had begun working part-time for the Air Ministry in 1936, while still continuing at Oxford, where he had studied under Professor Lindemann at the Clarendon Laboratory. Three years later, Fred Winterbotham, unable to cope with the amount of technical intelligence coming into his office, asked Sir Henry Tizard, head of the Committee for the Scientific Survey of Air Defence, whether he had a scientist who could help him. Sir Henry thought he had 'just the young man' and sent along Dr Jones, whom one newspaper later called the 'most famous practical joker in the scientific world'.

Jones already had a long list of practical jokes behind him. For instance, there was the trick he played on an eminent Ph.D. in Oxford. He began by ringing up the man several times and hanging up as soon as he answered. Some time later he telephoned again and pretended to be a Post Office engineer; there had been a report there was something wrong with the victim's telephone.

The victim readily agreed and Jones, as a Post Office engineer, said he'd send someone around to have a look at the phone—in a week's time.

'A week's time,' the victim exclaimed. 'That's awful. Can't you do better than that?'

Jones replied that it was impossible to send a repair-man at once as the Post Office was short-staffed; however, there was something the victim himself might be able to do. 'It may just be a leak to earth,' he explained. 'In that case we could fix it from here. It might be possible to find out whether it is, if you'd care to co-operate.'

The victim had been prepared.

'Well, first tap the telephone with something. A fountain pen, say, and let me hear the sound. That's right . . . Hmmm . . . can't tell. What kind of shoes are you wearing? Rubber heels? Ah yes, well, that's it. You'll have to take your shoes off, if you don't mind.'

Thereafter Jones had led his victim through a series of undignified manoeuvres until he finally decided that he could not 'repair' the phone.

'Oh no, please,' the other man had exclaimed. 'If there's anything else I can do, I'd like to try it.'

'Well, all right then. It's a crude approximation of a test we do with our own equipment. You have to get a bucket of water and lower the telephone into it, slowly.'

The hoax ended with the eminent Ph.D. standing shoeless, slowly lowering his phone into a bucket of water.

Although Jones's behaviour seemed very juvenile to many, the strange scientist's concept of the hoax was to stand him in good stead in the tragicomic world of the SIS in the years to come. As he explained his theory years later: 'With some hoaxes, the period of induction of the victim may be extended. In this type, which is probably the most interesting philosophically, the object is to build up in the victim's mind a false world-picture, which is temporarily consistent by any tests that he can apply to it, so that he ultimately takes action on it with confidence. The falseness of the picture is then starkly revealed by the incongruity which his action precipitates.'

But in November, 1939, when he told his new colleagues in the SIS that he believed in the authenticity of the mysterious 'Oslo Report', it was their opinion that the great hoaxster had himself fallen victim of a 'false world-picture'.

The whole strange business had started with an anonymous note to the British naval attaché in Oslo, asking him if he was interested in top-level scientific intelligence from Germany. If he was, the 'well-wishing German scientist' who had written the note would expect a slight change in the format of the BBC European News. The change was carried out and on 4 November, 1939, a parcel was put into the Embassy's letterbox.[1]

The package was sent to London, where Jones was to open it. 'I wondered whether it might contain a bomb that would

[1] Professor Jones writes of that anonymous well-wisher in a letter to the author: 'Various post-war claims have been made to me regarding the authorship of the Report, but I have found them unconvincing. I have my own ideas, but I would not publish them even at this stage'. My own guess is that it was the same scientist, an Austrian and editor of a topflight German scientific magazine, who in 1942 began supplying the British with details of German atomic bomb research, using the same country, Norway, to transmit his key material, this time, however, via the Norwegian underground.

explode on opening.' But the only bomb the parcel contained was the wealth of the top-secret information the enclosed report listed.

It gave a brief account of the two types of German radar, the Henschel 293 remote-control glider bomber, the German directional radio *Knickebein*, radio range-finding and a radio-controlled or gyrostabilized 'rocket shell' being tested for use against the Maginot line. The place where those tests were being carried out—Peenemuende! Jones 'found the text of the Report convincing from the start'. But no one else did. 'All the copies that went out to other departments were ignored', even the details of the 'wireless-controlled Henschel 293 being tried out there [Peenemuende] for use against ships under its secret number FZ 21 [*Ferngesteuertes Zielflugzeug*—remote-controlled target-plane]'. No one seemed concerned by that high number or the nature of the experiments being carried out with remote-controlled planes with lower code-numbers.[2] They should have been, for the Germans had already been working on the 50-foot, 13-ton, A-4 long-range rocket at Peenemuende for three years when Dr Jones received the mysterious 'Oslo Report'.

Thus the Report was shelved, though as Jones said later, 'As the war progressed and one development after another actually appeared, it was obvious that the Report was largely correct and in the few dull moments of the war, I used to look up the Oslo Report to see what should be coming along next.'

But as 1939 gave way to 1940 there were 'few dull moments' for him. As the German raids on Britain grew heavier, he came to the conclusion that the enemy was using pairs of directional beams from the Continent to guide their bombers and locate their targets. A lot of people disagreed with him, but Lindemann, now Churchill's principal scientific adviser, arranged for him to see the Prime Minister.

As Churchill himself described that meeting: 'For twenty minutes or more he spoke in quiet tones, unrolling his chain of circumstantial evidence, the like of which for its convincing fascination was never surpassed by tales of Sherlock

[2] The Henschel finally flew in September, 1943.

Holmes or Monsier Lecoq. As I listened the Ingoldsby Legends jingled in my mind:

> But now one Mr Jones
> Comes forth and depones
> That, fifteen years hence, he had heard certain groans
> On his way to Stonehenge to examine the stones. . . .'

Dr Jones sold the idea to Churchill. He ordered a plane with detection equipment to be sent up over a point in Derby where Jones reckoned the beams could most probably be located. The Air Ministry was not convinced and Jones knew his career was finished if he made a mistake now. However, 'it went like a dream. The detector plane went up and it found the beam just where I said it would be.'

His reputation made, Jones now employed his full talents as a hoaxster. Instead of jamming the beams as anyone without his slightly twisted imagination would, Jones duplicated them with the result that hundreds of tons of German bombs were dropped on empty fields.

By this time the British were using their own directional beam H2S, in particular against German submarines. Jones knew that the enemy would soon tumble to it and decided it was up to him to persuade them the British were employing some other device. Accordingly he 'invented' an infra-red beam, feeding the information back to them through the 'Double Cross Organization' (enemy agents caught in England, turned and now employed by the SIS). Jones even produced an infra-red picture of a ship taken from the air and made sure that the Germans received a copy.

The hoax was completely successful. The *Kriegsmarine* scientists even went as far as to invent a special paint which did not reflect infra-red rays and coated all the U-boats with it.

As the war progressed Jones went from strength to strength. He recommended the paradrop attack on the Bruneval radar station in France in order to capture secret German equipment. After a gliderborne force attempting to raid the German heavy water plant in Norway had been wiped out, he advised that a second raid (successful) should be executed by British-trained Norwegian saboteurs. Once he even managed to get the plans for a 1,000 bomber raid on Germany changed at the last moment.

But he still had nagging doubts about the research being done at Peenemuende. For by 1943 more and more alarming reports were coming out of Twelveland. But let us quote the 'most secret' *Air Scientific Intelligence Interim Report* of that year, which was the basis of all further action on the missile problem. Under *Secret Intelligence Reports December 1942–March 1943*, it reports:[3]

'3.1. On 18.12 a new source sent the first of three reports which when integrated provide the following account. In the three days beginning 30.11.42 Professor Fauner of the Berlin Technische Hochschule and an Engineer Szenassy had witnessed trials near Swinemuende (30 miles S.E. of Peenemuende) of a rocket containing 5 tons of explosive with a range of 200 kms and a danger area of 10kms square; it had automatic steering.

3.2. It is worth noting that while there is no Professor Fauner known to us, there are two professors, one Forner and the other Volmer of the BTH. The former is a specialist in steam turbine construction and the latter in physico-chemical thermodynamics, so that either might be easily associated with rocket development. Volmer has a son-in-law named Stransky who might possibly have become converted into the Szenassy reported . . .

3.3. A sub-source stated that the rocket was made at the Opel works at Ruesselsheim but unfortunately further details are precluded by his now being imprisoned for immoral practices.'

The report then turned to 'recent secret intelligence', which had been received 'subsequent to the focussing of attention on the Peenemuende rocket trials'. In particular, it based its findings on:

3 I am indebted to Mr David Irving for a copy of this report.

'7.3. The third source (also 2.6.43), a Luxembourger conscripted into the German Army, had been at Peenemuende and assisted at trials of a torpedo from 20.11.42 onwards. The torpedo was made at a nearby factory and started by catapult. It was said to be motor-driven and released over the beach with 'the noise of a squadron at low altitude'.

'7.4. The fourth source (5.6.43) was also a Luxembourger, whose report not only contained more detail but moreover agreed closely with photographic evidence. He said that long-range rockets were made at a factory at Peenemuende and mounted for firing upon a cubical contrivance containing gas bottles for initial propulsion. This gas was also made on the site. Rails 7–8 metres wide ran from assembly hall to firing range, the projectile revolved around its axis for 50 kms, when it commenced to wobble and deviate to the right. This problem was the most difficult to overcome. The range was certainly 150 possibly 250 kms. Plans from this source are to follow.'

The two reports had reached London and, if Dr Jones had really understood them, would have given Intelligence all it needed to know of the new threat from Twelveland.

2

TWO LADS FROM LUXEMBOURG

The whole business began when Pierre Ginter was expelled from Luxembourg City's *Goetheschule* because he refused to join the Hitler Youth. Since 1940, the citizens of the tiny principality which had been independent of Prussian domination since 1867, had been regarded by their German occupiers as *Reichsdeutsche* and thus required to serve the Reich. But Ginter, whose name was as German as his dialect, did not agree. He subscribed to the national motto, which stated in *'Letzeburger'* dialect 'We want to be left alone'. Unfortunately—for the Germans—the occupiers would not leave them alone. Thus when the Germans called him up in 1942 to do his six months *Arbeitsdienst* [Labour Service] Ginter crossed the border with hatred in his heart. Eventually he arrived in Berlin and was posted to the top-secret experimental station at Peenemuende.

On 18 October, 1942, he was paraded with his comrades to welcome the prima donna of the Third Reich 'Marshal of the Reich' Hermann Goering who was coming to inspect the firing of one of the new hush-hush 'aerial torpedoes'. But the torpedo exploded prematurely and the visit was cancelled. Pierre Ginter spent the day sweeping up the debris. A month later the captain in charge of the conscripts assembled them and announced proudly: 'Here we are going to manufacture the wonder weapons which will bring England to her knees'. When he told them that they 'will be missiles capable of flying three hundred to four hundred kilometres,' Ginter merely laughed.

A week later, however, Ginter's grin was wiped from his face when he saw one of the white-painted A-4 missiles make a perfect take-off. This time it flew off into the far distance, landing as their C.O. maintained later 'in the Bay of Danzig' several hundred kilometres away.

The incident gave Ginter cause for thought. Mentally he compared the distance allegedly flown by the 'aerial torpedo' with the distance across the English Channel. The matter puzzled him sufficiently for him to mention it in a round-about way in a letter to his pal, Camille Sutor, who had remained behind in Luxembourg. Camille, although only 19, was sufficiently smart to write back and advise Pierre to 'take a good look at everything'.[1]

Ginter decided he would do more than look; he would find the plans of the Peenemuende station. He decided that the place to find them would be in the *Arbeitsdienst* company office and volunteered for night telephone duty. The German sergeant was surprised.

Ginter explained, 'I've got a lot of letters to write and in our barrack room the lights go out at 9.30. The only way I can write them is to do telephone duty.'

The NCO was satisfied and gave him telephone duty for the next night.

At ten o'clock that night Ginter settled down in the office, his writing paper spread out in front of him on the desk as camouflage. But he did not get much time to 'write his letters home'. Every couple of minutes, German officers entered to ask him to find a number for them, usually those of their girl friends.

Around midnight things started to quieten down and he decided it was time to look for the plans. Idly he picked up a copy of the National Socialist periodical *Das Reich*, which lay in front of him on the desk. Beneath it were the office keys!

Without a second's hesitation he started to open all the cupboards he could find. He found soap, maps, formulae, spare food, but no plans. He had just opened the first of a series of low cupboards which ran round the floor of

---

[1] In these years Peenemuende security was very slack, although Hitler had already exclaimed 'God help us if the enemy finds out about this.' In a letter to the author, A. Speer, Hitler's key Minister of Armament, maintains that it was virtually impossible to prevent espionage on account of the many millions of foreign workers in German industry although he 'warned Hitler of the danger'.

the office and begun to rummage in it when the door opened.

A German officer looked at him severely and snapped: 'What are you doing?'

Ginter pulled himself together and tried a bold front; he knew what the *Reichsdeutsche* thought of the people they called *Beutedeutsche* ('looted Germans'): 'I'm stealing from the Reich Labour Service,' he said boldly.

'What!'

'Yes, I'm looking for more writing paper.' He indicated the paper-strewn desk. 'Mine's run out and I've got a lot of letters to answer.'

His boldness paid off. 'I see,' the officer said impatiently. 'All right, but now get me this number.'

While the German sat on the desk, swinging one booted leg, Ginter wrote carefully in a hand which trembled slightly: '*Meine liebe Mutter*.'

At last the officer left and Ginter was able to complete his search of the cupboard. It contained the sought-after plans and Ginter spent the rest of the night copying them into his notebook. But he could not complete the task that night and volunteered once again for telephone duty in order to finish copying the plans, as well as the site's anti-aircraft defences, down to the numbers of the individual guns.

On 2 January, 1943, Ginter returned to Luxembourg. He met Camille Sutor the next day and told him proudly, 'I've brought some beautiful things with me.' Camille was full of enthusiasm after leafing through the notebooks. 'We've got to get this to London,' he said, and urged Ginter to fill out his own notes and sketches so that the authorities in England would be able to understand them.[2]

On 8 January, 1943, Ginter finished and passed them on to Sutor who contacted a certain Dr Schwachtgen who,

[2] Camille Sutor was shot trying to resist arrest in 1944 when the Gestapo were searching his home where he had hidden a Canadian pilot. Ginter, in order to avoid conscription into the *Wehrmacht*, went underground for eighteen months and survived the war. Today he is the owner of a textile factory and burgomaster of the little Luxembourg town of Fels.

under the name of *Jean L'Aveugle*, was the head of the Luxembourg resistance organization, which had been formed by an Austrian Jewish member of the *Deuxième Bureau* named Gauthier Martin and had become part of the Northern French group entitled *Famille Martin*.

As we shall see, Schwachtgen tumbled to the significance of what Ginter had seen much sooner than many of the great 'scientific brains' back in London. He recalled a series of articles he had read before the war on space travel, published in a monthly named *Die Bergstadt* and guessed that the 'torpedo' Ginter described was really a space missile. He realized that the 'Ginter Report' was of vital importance and had five copies made of it, one for himself and four to be smuggled out by different routes to London.

Thereupon the doctor ordered his network to give first priority to obtaining information from Peenemuende; by now there were fifty young Luxembourgers working in the place, all of whom were writing regularly to their parents.

But Fernand Schwachtgen's time was running out. On 8 October, two German policemen appeared at his mother's home, where he was then living, to inform him that he was also to be deported to Upper Silesia on account of his anti-German attitude. They came at a very inopportune time for Schwachtgen had just prepared a parcel of secret information for one of his couriers who was to smuggle it into France that afternoon. What if the Germans searched the house?

Offering the policemen a meal, he excused himself while he went to tell his mother to prepare it. He seized the opportunity to hide the parcel in the outflow pipe of the toilet and then returned to his guests and the meal his mother had cooked for them. But Schwachtgen had not reckoned with the results of that meal. After he had finished eating one of the policemen excused himself to go to the lavatory.

Schwachtgen spent a very unpleasant five minutes, standing by the open window ready to spring out of it if the policeman returned with the parcel that could take him to the executioner's block. But when the policeman returned, buckling up his belt, his face bore the happy smile of a man who was well pleased with the world and himself.

A few moments later, as the police were leaving, Schwachtgen's mother appeared with the local burgomaster's secretary, Nicholas Kugener. The surprised clerk had just been walking up to the door when a parcel had suddenly appeared in the outflow pipe. Fortunately Madame Schwachtgen had spotted him, taken the parcel from him and hidden it beneath her apron.

But that was Jean L'Aveugle's last consignment of information. He was deported to the remote German province where he was later arrested on suspicion of espionage.[3] Thus the urgent message from London to the clandestine Parisian radio receiver 'Athos', which, unknown to Schwachtgen would help betray him, ordering 'Remind Jean L'Aveugle about Peenemuende', never reached him. Jean L'Aveugle was to spend many months of anxiety, wondering whether the OSS had received the vital information about Peenemuende.

It had, and not only from him. For there was another young Luxembourg agent already working in Peenemuende, unknown to Schwachtgen. He was 20-year-old Henri Roth, the son of a Wiltz railwayman who, like Pierre Ginter, had been ordered to do his service with the *Arbeitsdienst*, although he was already suspected of being a member of the Resistance.[4]

The young man's espionage career in Peenemuende started harmlessly enough with a letter dated 27 October, 1942, which he sent to his father, Leon. It arrived in Wiltz with a white strip attached to the envelope stating that it had been opened by the censor. The railwayman soon found out why—half the second page had been detached and on the third page his son's place of employment had been neatly blackened out.

[3] He survived.
[4] The Germans' lack of security up to 1943 at the top secret research station is beyond comprehension. Indeed, the fact that the two Luxembourgers could obtain the information so easily was one of the arguments used in some quarters to maintain that the whole missile business was a German 'plant'.

Another father might have dismissed the matter but Leon Roth was the main courier between Luxembourg and Belgium for the Belgian 'White Army' resistance force and a member of the network which smuggled Belgian and French POWs out of Germany after their escape.

In the summer of 1942, Roth had also made contact with another Belgian group, the *'Service Clarence'*, organized by a policeman named Adolphe Godart. He was given the code-name 'Oscar 8353' and ordered to obtain information about German war factories in Wiltz. Thus it was that at his next meeting with Godart—'Pierre 8360'—he mentioned his son's censored letter. Godart contacted London and was informed that it was of the greatest importance to find out where young Roth was employed. The wheel had started to turn.

At this time Henri Roth did not know that his father was a spy. All the same he did not want his letters to be censored again, so he started to post them from the nearby town of Zinnowitz.

His very next letter created a minor sensation in the 'Clarence' network, for it contained not only a sketch map of the Usedom set-up but also said that experiments were being carried out there with 'an aerial torpedo, which moves under its own power and makes a noise as if a squadron of heavy bombers were approaching'. Slightly garbled, that same description was to turn up in Jones' most secret report to Mr Churchill in July 1943. 'The torpedo . . . was said to be motor driven and released over the beach with the noise of a squadron at low altitude.'

Roth's letters continued to be a very valuable source of information for the SIS. Indeed 'Pierre 8360' and his deputy, 'Hubert 8362', used to come to the Belgian frontier personally to collect them from Leon. Leon always refused to give them the originals. He kept them hidden in a safe place. The two agents received copies, which Leon hoped might save his son if 'Pierre' and 'Hubert' were captured.

When Henri Roth returned from Peenemuende in 1943, the RAF 'Moonlight Squadron', the SIS's own agent-dropping force, offered to collect him from a secret air strip near the village of Sure. Henri declined. If the Gestapo discovered he was gone, his father and family would suffer. He stayed and died the unknown death of so many young men like him in those years.[5]

[5] Already under suspicion, he thought service in the German forces would be the best way to 'go underground' without endangering his family. For a while he served in Russia before being transferred to the cruiser *Admiral Scheer*. At the end of March, 1945, the *Scheer* was torpedoed, but Roth was not among the survivors. According to the *Scheer*'s captain, named Pruetzmann, Roth had deserted on 20 March. That was all the British authorities or Leon Roth could find out.

3

THE FAILURE

On the same day, 29 June, 1943, that Peenemuende succeeded in firing two A-4s without a hitch, Churchill called together the Cabinet's Defence Committee to discuss what should be done about the Peenemuende problem.

The underground Cabinet War Room, which was reputed to be the most complex command centre in the whole of Europe was crowded with the country's civilian and military leaders—Attlee, Eden, Beaverbrook, Morrison—as well as the members of Sandys' committee which had been appointed to investigate the danger presented by the German experimental station.

Duncan Sandys opened the meeting with a dramatic discussion of the 'white-painted rockets' photographed at Peenemuende. He was convinced that Peenemuende constituted a major threat to Britain's home front.

Herbert Morrison, the man in charge of that front, wasn't. Morrison felt that the SIS reports were too numerous for such a top-secret German undertaking. Information such as that which had come from the two young Luxembourgers was surely a 'plant'. Mr Sandys countered that the flood of intelligence was due to the drive he had ordered at SIS a few weeks back.

Professor Lindemann, now Lord Cherwell, also launched an aggressive attack on Sandys' intelligence information and suggested that the whole business was an 'elaborate cover plan' aimed at covering up some other sinister German machination.

Churchill felt that his principal scientific adviser's technical points were worthy of closer consideration. Without further ado he turned to the youngest man present, introduced his past record of scientific intelligence and said: 'Now Dr Jones, may we hear the *truth!*'

Jones demolished Cherwell's arguments one by one, introducing a new intelligence source to back up his evidence—a German Army officer in Major-General Leyer's *Waffenamt* [weapons department] who had passed on the information from Berlin that Hitler had demanded that the rockets should be put into action as soon as possible.

In the end Jones won the day. It was decided that an intensive intelligence and air reconnaissance programme should be put in hand and that 'the attack on the experimental station should take the form of the heaviest possible night attack by Bomber Command on the first occasion when conditions were suitable and that in the meanwhile undue aerial reconnaissance of the place should be avoided'.

Thus the meeting broke up with Jones knowing that the SIS would have to redouble its efforts, now that aerial reconnaissance had been virtually forbidden. What he didn't realise was that he had made a powerful enemy in Lord Cherwell.

As the civil authorities started making preparations for the threatened mystery attack, the intelligence reports from Twelveland kept flooding into SIS HQ: the body of a rocket spotted by an agent at Hanover station; a whole consignment of them noted by Polish agents at the Leipzig marshalling yards; two reports from spies who had seen rockets launched from aircraft; the rockets were calculated to weigh up to ten tons. But still Lord Cherwell set his face against the threat posed by weapons that the SIS had discovered at Peenemuende. As late as 29 July, he was still writing: 'I am biased by the fact that I do not believe in the rocket's existence.'

Sixteen days later, however, the weather was thought suitable for 'Bomber' Harris's Lancasters and Halifaxes to attack the experimental station. Feigning a raid on Berlin and aided by two renegade Germans in the Arnhem-Deelen German Fighter Control Centre who misdirected the German fighter defence, Harris took Peenemuende by complete surprise.

153

By six o'clock on the morning of the 19th German sources reported that Peenemuende was burning from end to end. When Colonel-General Hans Jeschonnek, the *Luft-waffe's* Chief-of-Staff heard the news he shot himself, leaving behind a note saying: 'I cannot work with Goering any more. Long live the Führer!'

Thereafter the Germans started to disperse some of the most important experimental sections of the devastated plant to the Harz mountains, central Poland and Southern Germany. As a consequence the great German attack did not develop. Cherwell, confident that there had been nothing in Jones's long range rocket theory, inclined more and more to believe that the Germans were really trying to develop a kind of glider bomb, one that would have a limited speed and fly at the same altitude as a normal plane. A rocket-bomb of this type could be shot down by conventional fighter planes or anti-aircraft fire.

On 12 June, 1944, the first four 'doodle bugs' landed in southern England and Cherwell felt that his theory was vindicated. Jones went to see him at once. Cherwell chuckled, 'The mountain hath groaned and given forth a mouse!'

Jones was horrified. He reminded his former teacher of the firing trials at Peenemuende reported by the SIS. In his opinion, the Germans were capable of a much bigger effort than this. 'For God's sake,' he entreated Cherwell, 'don't laugh this one off!'

Now Jones sought desperately for some way of convincing Churchill and Cherwell that there was a far bigger threat hovering over Britain than the one ton flying bomb, the V-1. He turned his attention to Blizna to which the Germans had evacuated much of their A-4 programme. He ordered fresh air reconnaissance of the area, but he knew that he would need more than photographic evidence to convince his opponents that the Germans were planning a large-scale heavy-rocket attack, which would be impervious to conventional anti-aircraft and fighter defence. He was beginning to despair of ever being able to change the minds of his superiors when two things happened—a V-2 crashed in southern Sweden after refusing to obey the signals beamed at it from Peenemuende and the Polish intelligence service based in western Poland and Germany provided him with a stolen V-2 or at least its vital parts!

4

HOW TO STEAL A SECRET WEAPON

The first indication that something unusual was taking place in the remote wooded area around the Polish town of Blizna came from Polish agents in Saxony. They reported that a long goods train of what looked like aeroplane parts was on its way to Poland. The headquarters of the Polish Home Army noted the matter, but thought nothing more of it.

At the end of 1943, however, three German civilians, driving through the Warsaw suburb of Praga, had a serious accident and were delivered into a nearby Polish hospital, where they died a few hours later. But before they passed away they were visited by several high-ranking German officials who expressed regret in the presence of the Polish nurses at the loss of these 'indispensable' men.

The remark was passed on to the Polish Intelligence and they found it interesting enough to set one of their specialists, an engineer named Antoni Kocjan, to discover what was so important about the dead men. Kocjan's spy at Blizna soon discovered that strange things were happening there. Every morning a plane appeared above the woods which surrounded the place, circled once and then disappeared. Thereafter there was a great droning sound and a projectile flew into the air to disintegrate with a tremendous crash. A few days later the spy hid himself at the station of Kochanowka from which a new branch line ran off to Blizna, and saw what looked like a consignment of aeroplane parts from Breslau rumbling up the new stretch of track.

Immediately Kocjan contacted the Polish Intelligence agents in Breslau, who reported that the parts had not come from there. A few days later, Kocjan learned that a strange German plane had crashed at Lublin and disintegrated. Not a trace of the plane or the crew had been found. If that weren't curious enough, the Germans had insisted on measuring up the whole site where the plane had crashed and a high-ranking German officer had actually *apologized* to the local Polish population for the 'accident' and said he was prepared to pay for any damage incurred.

After four years of German occupation, Kocjan knew he was onto something: the strange shipments from an unknown destination within the Reich, a mysterious plane blowing up without trace near Lublin and the curious tests at Blizna. Then he received yet another report of mysterious German experiments. It came from an engineer whose brother was employed by a brewery at Sarnaki, a small place nearly a hundred miles from Warsaw. Tadeusz Korczik, the man in question, reported that a German officer had been billeted in the brewery with forty soldiers. Every morning he and his men took up their position at a look-out post in the old Jewish cemetery, where they reported to Cracow by radio. A couple of minutes later the whole village would be shaken by a tremendous explosion. It was as if 'a plane had exploded in mid-air'.

The Polish engineer in charge of the Intelligence Service investigation decided it was time that he had a personal look at the whole strange business. He took the train to Sarnaki.

On the very first morning after his arrival in the tumbledown village, the house in which he was hiding was indeed shaken by a tremendous explosion, as if 'a plane had exploded in mid-air'.

Hurriedly, before the Germans could drive from their command post to pick up the pieces, Kocjan ran out into the fields and began to stuff lumps of glass wool, bits of bakelite and pieces of metal into his pockets. Day after day the same thing happened. The engineer and his helpers flooded the Warsaw HQ with bits and pieces of the strange weapons, in spite of German threats and rewards for any material surrendered to them—a litre bottle of vodka.

But the peasants continued to dispatch everything they found so that by the turn of the year the Polish intelligence men in Warsaw could safely conclude that the things fired at Blizna, which dropped in a 30 square mile area around Sarnaki, were not some kind of glider bomb or pilotless aeroplane. They were obviously some type of ultra secret weapon, for even *German* planes were not allowed to fly over Blizna. The Poles' conclusion was supported by frantic radio messages from London asking them to try to obtain parts of an intact object, whatever it might be.

At the end of May, 1944, a farmer named Jan Lopaciuk, who lived in the village of Klimczyce close to Sarnaki, ran into Dr Marian Korczik's surgery and reported breathlessly that one of the strange objects had dived into a marsh on the banks of the River Bug and failed to explode. Tadeusz Korczik, the doctor's brother, left his office in the local brewery at once and ran across the fields to the spot where the object had landed. Having photographed it, he ordered the gawping farmers who were standing around the white-painted missile to push it deeper into the water and cover it with reeds.

And there the secret weapon remained while the Germans searched for it for three whole days without success. As soon as they broke off their search, the Poles went to work. The larger parts of the rocket were buried deeper in the water, but its nose was dismantled and sent to Warsaw where the scientists employed by the Polish Intelligence Service decided that the contents of the nose were so important that they had to be smuggled out to London immediately.

London agreed and radioed that a Dakota would fly from the SOE base at Brindisi in southern Italy to pick up the vital parts as soon as the Poles had found a suitable landing place. That problem was soon solved—a little meadow near Tarnow, a village not too far from the River Vistula.

But there was another problem, not solved so easily. Poland was flooded with German troops retreating from the advancing Red Army. How were the Poles going to transport the vital parts across the country to the spot they had picked for the plane, which was several hundred miles away, and not be discovered?

Kocjan, who was in charge of the whole operation, decided that the nose's individual parts should be concealed in compressed air cylinders, which would later be rewelded and the welds painted over. Kocjan was satisfied with the finished job; the cylinders looked as if they would stand up to examination by any suspicious German military policeman. He radioed Brindisi that he was ready to go ahead with the operation. The job of transporting the cylinders went off without a hitch. None of the retreating Germans seemed interested in the Poles and their rickety truck. The Poles took up their hiding places in the surrounding villages and waited for the Dakota.

But then an unexpected hitch arose. A German plane landed on the meadow, which had been a pre-war emergency landing field for the Polish Air Force, and crashed on landing. A couple of days later two German Army spotter planes landed there too. If that weren't bad enough, a small German *Luftwaffe* unit set up camp about one kilometre from the landing site. Obviously, the Poles realized, the Germans were going to use the meadow as a frontline landing strip as soon as the Russians reached the area.

What were they to do?

The decision was made for them. On the evening of 26 July, SOE HQ at Brindisi radioed that the Dakota was on its way. It would land on the meadow at about midnight. The Poles had no choice but to go ahead and fight it out if necessary. But luck was on their side. Just as the sun was setting the two German planes took off, followed a little later by the small German *Luftwaffe* unit. The meadow was theirs.

Punctually at midnight the Dakota made a perfect touchdown. The Poles sneaked from the shadows and started loading the precious cargo. Within thirty minutes the plane was loaded and its passengers safely aboard. The pilot switched on the engines and opened the throttle but nothing happened! The motors roared but the plane did not move. The Dakota's wheels had sunk into the mud and were stuck.

Pilot and passengers got out again. The pilot checked the brakes to see they were not blocked while the Poles cleared the wheels. Satisfied, they boarded the plane again. But still it refused to take off.

Marek Celt, now an exile from his native country, remembers the scene: 'We were terribly tense. The meadow was brightly lit by the plane's lights and the roar of the motors, heightened by the echo in the woods, could probably be heard as far as Tarnov. The Germans could come at any moment—they weren't very far from our meadow. We despaired. It had taken so much effort to arrange everything. We had waited for the plane for nearly two weeks and experienced many dangerous moments—and now everything was apparently to be in vain. I had a sack full of important communications for London with me and my comrades, whose loads remained a mystery to me, were in exactly the same position. All of us stood there as if we were mesmerized.'

But the passengers had not reckoned with the local farmers summoned by the Polish Intelligence men. While the latter freed the Dakota's wheels with their bare hands, the farmers brought up cartloads of wooden planks, ripped from the fences around their houses. These they shoved under the freed wheels and laid a track across the meadow.

Once again the passengers climbed aboard. The pilot turned on the engines. Slowly but surely the Dakota started to move forward. It gathered speed as it wobbled across the meadow. Seconds later it was airborne.

The arrival of the Polish parts, plus those from Sweden obtained by a secret deal with the Swedes involving two squadrons of British tanks,[1] helped Jones to convince the authorities that the V-2 was a real danger.

But still they were not prepared to act. Cherwell was not willing to believe that the Germans would spend so many years in researching a rocket which, in his opinion, would

---

[1] The German *Abwehr* tried to get through the lines of Swedes cordoning off the site of the unexploded rocket by pretending to be a burial party. The dodge failed. Now the British were winning, the Swedes were prepared to do business with them rather than with the Germans. Although Jones had suggested giving them Spitfires for the vital parts, the powers-that-be decided that tanks would be more suitable.

only be capable of delivering the same weight of explosive as the V-1.

In vain Jones tried to convince Cherwell and Churchill that the Germans probably had a store of some 1,500 rockets, with a monthly production of some 500 more per month. Britain could therefore expect an attack rate of about 800 rockets per month. Churchill turned on him; Sandys began to lose interest, and Morrison began to abandon his contingency plans to meet the possible new offensive.

On 4 August the RAF photo-reconnaissance section reported, after examining the now abandoned Blizna site, that they had discovered about twelve large conical objects. The photo-interpreters decided that there was a good 'possibility of their being firing bases shaped like lemon squeezers'.

Jones examined the photos himself and recognized the 'lemon squeezers' firing points for what they were—bell tents used to accommodate the Blizna ground crews. His sense of humour had not abandoned him. He sent an 'Air Scientific Intelligence: Tentative Report', basing it on the theory that one picture is better than a thousand words. It showed a 50-foot rocket perched on a bell tent. Three puzzled German soldiers were staring at it in amazement, one of them holding the 'lemon squeezer' report in his hand. The whole was labelled 'Geheime Kommandosache!' (top secret).

Two weeks later Jones presented his last report on the subject and it showed no evidence of humour. He put forward a well-reasoned, logical case for the action or non-action on the part of the authorities when Intelligence provided them with details of a new development. In his opinion four situations could arise in such a case:

'I. Neither side makes it work; this presents no Intelligence problem.

II. Both sides succeed; this is the normal Intelligence problem, for it soon becomes a matter of general knowledge and Intelligence is reasonably well briefed as to what to seek.

161

III. Our experts succeed, the Germans fail; this is an Intelligence worry, for proving the negative case is one of the most difficult of Intelligence exercises.
IV. Our experts fail, or do not try; the Germans succeed. This is the most interesting Intelligence case, but it is difficult to overcome the prejudice that as *we* have not done something, it is impossible or foolish.

Alternatively our experts, in examining the German development, are no longer experts but novices and many therefore make wilder guesses than Intelligence, which at least has the advantage of being in closer contact with the enemy.'

The report of 27 August, 1944, was widely circulated among the high-ranking military and civilian leaders concerned, but the sting in its tail was too obvious. After two days it was recalled and Jones retired from the battle to convince the authorities of the danger presented by the V-2.

Two weeks later Mr Morrison got Churchill's permission to suspend all evacuation from London. Duncan Sandys, a politician after all and concerned with his post-war prospects, went on record as saying that 'Except possibly for a few last shots, the Battle of London is over.' On the very next evening, the Germans launched the first V-2 at London from Holland. It was the first of 1,000 which fell before the last one landed on London in mid-March, 1945.

But Jones's sense of humour did not desert him some time later when the daughter of a director of the Bank of England, Constance Babington-Smith, was awarded a decoration for the first spotting of a V-weapon launching site in 1943. Considerable fuss was made of the new 'heroine' of the 'secret battle against the German horror weapons'—even the German-made lenses with which she had discovered the site were preserved for posterity. Jones, who felt that he had directed her, by his own calculations, to find that site, assumed his best lady journalist's voice and telephoned her, pretending to be a representative of a well-known female weekly. Would Miss Babington-Smith be ready to receive a photographer to take her picture for the next number? 'Like a queen,' as he described her reaction, she said she would be. But the photographer never turned up. As Professor Jones said years later, 'No doubt she is still waiting.'

PART THREE

STALEMATE

(1944)

'But if Intelligence was not to blame, who was?'

General Kenneth Strong,
Eisenhower's Chief-of-Intelligence.

1

BIG RED DOES BUSINESS WITH HIMMLER

On the day that the first V-2 dropped, Allen Dulles arrived in London on his way to Washington to confer with Donovan about the failure of the German generals to assassinate Hitler. Donovan also wanted to know what steps the OSS was going to take to penetrate Twelveland itself, now that American troops had reached the borders of the Reich.

Dulles was pleased with his first year of work in Europe. He had built an espionage organization from scratch— virtually every American working or stranded in Switzer- land had been approached—and had established solid con- tacts with the German resistance. He had obtained Wood's services and these had proved a mine of valuable informa- tion. Naturally Dulles did not know that his German con- tacts in the resistance were using 'the most influential White House man in Europe', as the Germans thought him, to drive a wedge between the Western Allies and the Russians, directly contrary to Roosevelt's instructions to Donovan. The President had told Donovan: 'Bill, you must treat the Russians with the same trust you do the British. They're killing Germans every day, you know.' Nor did he know that ninety per cent of the information he obtained through Wood was already known to the British.[1] In short Dulles was like an innocent child in the corrupt world of European intelligence.

Indeed Dulles was so confident that he knew everything

[1] The only real scoop Dulles achieved in 1943-4 was the information obtained from Wood that the German agent Cicero had burgled the safe of his master, the British ambassador in Turkey, and had stolen or photo- graphed key documents, including details of the coming D-Day invasion.

that was going on behind the scenes in Germany, thanks to Wood, that he had reported to Donovan a short time before: 'Sincerely regret you cannot at this time see Wood's material as it stands without condensation and abridgment. In some 400 pages, dealing with the internal manoeuvrings of German diplomatic policy for the past two months, a picture of imminent doom and final downfall is presented. Into a tormented General Headquarters and a half-dead Foreign Office stream the lamentations of a score of diplomatic posts. It is a scene wherein haggard Secret Service and diplomatic agents are doing their best to cope with the defeatism and desertion of flatly defiant satellites and allies and recalcitrant neutrals. The period of secret service under Canaris . . . is drawing to an end. Already Canaris has disappeared from the picture and a conference was hurriedly convoked in Berlin at which efforts were made to mend the gaping holes left in the *Abwehr*.'

Dulles' conclusion had been: 'The final death-bed contortions of a putrefied Nazi diplomacy are pictured in these telegrams.' Dulles was in for a great surprise when Nazi Germany showed that it was not ready to die just yet. But for the time being his surprise was limited to what he found in the Washington headquarters of the OSS that October.

Since he had left it in 1942, it had expanded tremendously to guide the destinies of the 30,000 OSS agents throughout the world. Its staff was heavy with prominent German refugees such as the political philosopher Herbert Marcuse whose theories rocked the student world from Berkeley to Berlin twenty odd years later; big businessmen eager to get to Europe to protect their business interests, such as Colonel Behn, head of the ITT corporation, who four years before had apparently believed that the Germans would win the war; American intellectuals of all shades of opinion from the deepest red to the purest blue; and even members of religious organizations who believed that German churchmen would make an ideal anti-Nazi resistance-spy ring.[2]

Dulles did not like what he saw. To him many of the

[2] Apparently they were unaware of the support the two major German religious denominations gave to Hitler, with pictures of bishops of both faiths giving the Hitler salute a commonplace in German papers.

schemes being hatched by the German and American 'eggheads' were just 'crackbrained'. Dutifully he did the rounds, picked up one or two new ideas and an instruction to see what he could do about infiltrating agents into Germany to help the advancing US armies, and then flew back to Switzerland via France, undoubtedly relieved to get out of the crazy atmosphere of the Washington 'head shed'.

To his surprise, he found he had an entirely new staff waiting for him. The OSS man in Zurich was now Russel D'Oench, a member of the Grace Shipping Line family. Geneva was run by William Mellon, son of the president of Gulf Oil. The two OSS agents watching the Swiss-Italian border were joined by the Russian emigre Valerian Lada-Mocarski, who had once sat with Dulles on the board of the Schroeder Bank, which had connections with ITT. It almost seemed as if Washington had accepted his report, based on Wood's spy-ring, in its entirety. The war was about over. Now it was time for big business to step in and try to pick up the pieces.

All the same Dulles knew that it was imperative to get agents into Germany to help the American armies belonging to Bradley's 12th Army Group, which were expected to make their big push into the Reich at any moment. The USAAF 8th Air Force in Britain was also crying out for details of German war plants, in particular those in the oil and ball-bearing industries, prime targets in the strategic bombing campaign.

Dulles conferred with his new staff and discovered that the OSS had only one agent in Germany, *and that agent was already a prisoner and a woman to boot*!

The woman in question, Virginia Hall, the first woman in the Second World War to win the Distinguished Service Cross, had been parachuted into Occupied France with an artificial leg tucked under her arm—she had lost her own leg in a motoring accident. She had taken part in sabotage together with the French Resistance and had helped to blow up a strategically important bridge, killing 150 Germans and winning the DSC.

Thereafter she had been posted to the OSS unit attached to General Bradley's HQ at Luxembourg. But she could not get used to headquarters life and one day borrowed a jeep to have 'a look at the frontline'. Unfortunately the jeep joyride had taken her into Germany itself, so she became the first American woman to be captured.[3]

Dulles ordered a crash operation. Sixteen 'volunteers'— a few Allied nationals but mostly 'turned' German POWs— were hurriedly trained at Namur and dropped into the Rhineland a month later. The plan was that they would locate themselves near important rail centres or industrial areas and begin to operate the new OSS communications device known as 'Joan-Eleanor' (J–E).

The 'J–E' was a tremendously expanded form of the 'Walkie-talkie', weighing about four pounds and using long-life batteries. It was easy to conceal and because of its high frequency and vertical cone-shaped directivity, it was virtually impossible for the mobile *Abwehr* detection teams to locate it.

The agent used it by contacting a specially adapted British Mosquito, containing a pilot and, in the nose, a radio operator, who at a height of 30,000 feet could ask the agent exactly what was going on on the ground. Unlike all clandestine radio communication systems used hitherto, the operator in the Mosquito, in direct two-way voice contact with the spy, could ask for further clarification, direct him closer to the target and, most important, obtain more information in a few minutes than would normally have been gained in a week of periodic radio transmissions.

But in spite of the new radio device with which they were equipped, the first batch of OSS agents dropped into the Reich proved a great disappointment. Only four succeeded in making contact with headquarters, the rest broke up their sets immediately once they had returned to the *Heimat* and presumably either surrendered to the police, fled to the safety of their families or were killed. And how they were killed!

'It was the boys who spotted him first hanging around in the meadows above the village,' Herr Ertz, today the

---

[3] Six months later she escaped and made her way back to Berne. From there she was flown back to Washington under conditions of great secrecy and her career with the OSS was over.

director of a German insurance company, but then a little boy in his home village of Oberkail in the Eifel, recalls:[4] 'That winter of forty-four was terrible, a lot of snow, so the men didn't take the cattle out to pasture. But the boys playing around the edges of the village after school saw him a couple of times in the trees. Mind you he was quick. As soon as he saw them looking his way, he was off like a shot.'

Oberkail was situated in a remote little valley in the Eifel hills some thirty miles as the crow flies from the US lines in Luxembourg. The GIs called it the 'ghost front'; nothing much ever happened there. All the same the Oberkail boys knew there was a war on and the ever-growing number of troops in the surrounding countryside, grouping there for the German surprise attack through the Ardennes, had made them spy-conscious. Indeed those of them old enough to be in the Hitler Youth were regularly sent on 'spy exercises' by their group leaders.

'Of course the boys thought the strange man in the fields was a spy straightaway. But the old folks in the village laughed at them at first. As you know, farmers are slow to move. When one of them, however, spotted the man staring at the village through binoculars the men changed their minds.

'In those days there was no gendarme in the village and the farmers didn't want to make themselves look foolish by contacting the nearest police post in Bitburg. So a bunch of them went off to look for the "spy" themselves, arming themselves with rakes and shovels and the usual sort of tools you'll find in a farmyard.' They found the 'spy' easily enough. He'd been out in the fields two days by this time and although he had dug himself a hole underneath some bushes and was warmly dressed, the necessity of being constantly on the alert had worn him down. He surrendered at once.

'He said he was an *Ami*, an American, though he spoke fluent High German. At first the farmers didn't know exactly what to do with him. After all it isn't every day that a group of country folk find a spy in their fields. But then after they found his radio, they started to grow angry. Today I can imagine the man couldn't really understand what they were

[4] In a conversation with the author.

talking about—they spoke their own dialect—but he could see from their faces that their intentions were not good. His face grew pale. Then somebody hit him with a shovel. He staggered and almost fell. Somebody else hit with a rake. This time he went down on his knees. I think he was bleeding by then. That really started them. After all they'd had a pretty bad time in the last few months with the American fighters machine-gunning them in the streets and their cattle in the fields. They worked off all their rage on the poor American. I couldn't stand it. I ran away. Later I heard they buried his body in the hole he had dug to hide himself.'

Thus the first OSS mission into Germany ended in desertion, disaster and violent death and the Americans, like their British allies four years before, were eyeless in Twelveland. It was time to reactivate 'Big Red'.

Erik Erickson had made his last trip to Germany in 1943, but now, with oil production being cut in the Reich, it was becoming increasingly difficult for him to find a plausible excuse to apply to enter the country. But when Wilko Tikander, an ex-Chicago lawyer who was now the head of OSS in Stockholm, called him and told him it was imperative he found out what was going on in the German synthetic oil industry, he set about trying to solve the problem.

At dinner the following evening, Erickson discussed the situation with Prince Carl and his new wife Ingrid, a Swedish beauty half his age. Prince Carl first suggested that he should try to convince the Germans to let him make a kind of morale-boosting tour of the oil industry. The Germans would be able to publish his picture at the various plants and thus convince the world all was well with the Third Reich. For his part it would be a convenient means of espionage.

Erickson vetoed the suggestion and made a counter-proposal sparked by his wife's statement that the Nazis were no longer interested in *selling* oil to Sweden but *obtaining* it from them. 'That's it!' he interrupted. 'We'll offer *them* oil. We'll pretend that we're going to build a huge synthetic refinery here in Sweden, where it'll be safe from bombs.' Prince Carl pointed out that, though the idea was good, it wouldn't get them into the Reich.

'Not so fast,' Erickson countered. 'First I have to survey *their* synthetic refineries and see the various types of equipment and techniques used so that I can decide which is best for us.' Prince Carl warmed to the idea and suggested that in order to convince the Germans that it was a bona fide scheme they should float a Swedish company to finance it.

Thus the great deception was born.

With Tikander's approval they began to recruit suitable Swedish backers—men like Lars Thulin, a director of the state-owned Farmers' Bank and Axel Edmar, a vice-president of the Swedish Co-operative Oil Association, whose name appeared in the prospectus they prepared for the Germans.[5] The publisher, Ture Nerman, an ex-communist who four years before had been a member of the SIS's Rickmann League, managed to steal a copy of the prospectus and created a scandal by publishing it in his papers. Although its publication, which showed there was virtually no co-operation between the SIS and OSS in Sweden, embarrassed a number of the new firm's backers, it did help to improve Erickson's standing with the local German community. Finally the Germans bit and in November, 1944, Erickson was invited to visit no other person than Heinrich Himmler himself to discuss the scheme. 'Operation Gasbag', as Tikander had nicknamed it, was under way.

[5] Afterwards Mr Erickson maintained that their names and others were forged to deceive the Germans. I shall leave it to the reader to decide, though one must point out that any Swedish businessman backing Germany in late '44 could not have been very perceptive.

2

OPERATION GASBAG NEARLY SPRINGS
A LEAK

Erickson met Himmler at his Berlin headquarters which had already suffered badly in the Allied bombing and would soon have to be abandoned altogether. The meeting began with some small talk, dominated naturally by the *Reichsführer*, who was once cynically characterized by one of his closest associates as a 'complete realist with his two feet planted squarely one metre above the ground!' Finally, however, Erickson managed to bring him round to discussing the proposed Swedish oil plant.

Larding his argument with 'as you know' and 'as you will no doubt recall', which he calculated would flatter Himmler, Erickson listed the advantages of the Swedish project: it would show the world that one neutral—Sweden —believed in Germany's ultimate victory; it would be an ideal means of investing the SS funds which were under Himmler's control;[1] and it would supply the *Wehrmacht* with badly needed oil.

Although all these details were included in Erickson's prospectus, he had long realized that important men never read anything; they wanted to hear. And Himmler seemed to like what he heard. He digressed several times, however. Once he asked, 'What would happen if the *Wehrmacht* were to invade Sweden?'

Erickson answered promptly: 'The Swedes would fight

[1] For several years, influential German industrialists—'Friends of the *Reichsführer SS*', as they called themselves—had been donating money to the SS. In October, 1944, Himmler held a mysterious meeting with his 'Friends' in Strasbourg apparently to decide what should be done with the vast funds at his disposal. Thereafter nothing more was heard of them. Were they invested in overseas firms, as has often been suggested? Are they in Swiss banks? No one knows.

like hell!' Then before Himmler could go off at a tangent again, he rammed home the real purpose of his visit. 'There is one thing, *Reichsführer*,' he said. 'I am myself not an expert on synthetic oil production[2] and I think it would really be best if I saw the different types of operations at first hand. Then I will know just what is required in the way of equipment and personnel, and I'll be able to plan the most efficient production set-up.'

Himmler, the chief of a counter-intelligence organization numbering 30,000 men never even suspected the salesman-spy. Before Erickson left his headquarters that day he had been provided with passes on Himmler's express orders, granting him permission to inspect Germany's refineries and enter the Reich's *Sperrgebiete* (restricted areas). The first part of Operation Gasbag had gone off without a hitch.

On the third day of his amazing tour of the German oil industry, Erickson began to suspect that he was being followed. It was the first time that this had happened to him in his four years of operations in Nazi Germany. He tried his usual trick of meeting his contacts in a brothel and although the man followed him inside, he did not see Erickson discuss vital secret information with his Hanover contact. Erickson thought he had shaken him off.

But two days later, after he had inspected the Bohlen refinery outside Leipzig, he was hailed in the street by a German who he had known in pre-war days; and his erst-while business rival was exceedingly suspicious.

Erickson tried to disarm him by inviting him for a drink, but the German remained suspicious. 'I would have expected you to be in Texas or somewhere pulling off some deals for Standard for your British friends,' he persisted.

Erickson plied the man with more drinks and told the German that for him 'business was business'; he didn't care who won the war as long as his deals didn't suffer in the process.

The German changed his tack and asked Erickson what he was doing in Leipzig. Grateful for the respite, Erickson explained that he was there on a special project which had

[2] At this time 35 per cent of Germany's oil was manufactured synthetically.

the blessing of the *Reichsführer SS* himself. The German listened in silence and then asked if Erickson would mind showing him his credentials. Erickson obliged and the man seemed satisfied. All the same 'Big Red', as he was nicknamed in OSS circles, knew that he was not out of danger yet. As he explained to the Swedish press when his full story was revealed, the suspicious German businessman might well reveal his pre-war antagonism to fascism to the local Gestapo. The German obviously had a lot of contacts in high places and, in the tense atmosphere of the Reich after the abortive attempt on Hitler's life in the previous July, it did not take much to have someone arrested and 'liquidated'. So Erickson decided that there was only one way out of his dilemma: *he would have to get rid of the German!*

After saying good-bye, Erickson went back to his hotel and dodged out of the back entrance to throw off any Gestapo 'tail'. Then, hailing a taxi, he hurried after his victim, finally catching up with him as he stepped into a telephone booth. Whether the German was intending to telephone the Gestapo or not, Erickson never found out. But he wasn't taking any chances; his own life was at stake.

He opened the glass door, knife in hand. In the blue-lit booth no one could see him from outside. The knife flashed. The German gave one stifled groan. A few moments later he slumped over the phone, dead.

In spite of the shock occasioned by the murder, Erickson carried on a few days more, touring Halle and Merseburg and moving from there to the south as far as Sigmaringen, the home of the Vichy Government—or what was left of it. From there he travelled north again, via Berchesgrend, a new industrial complex, to Berlin, the end of his journey.

His report, filed with Wilko Tikander later, gave a comprehensive account of his travels, which was highly informative for the 8th USAAF Targets Section. In part, it read: 'Annendorf—rebuilt as a synthetic plant after the demolishing of the Leuna plant at Halle. The plant does not lie exactly at the Annendorf station, but is about 15km north of Merseburg quite close to the RR on the route Halle-

Annendorf. The plant is on the left side of the RR and is gigantic (Map attached).

'Leuna at Halle and Merseburg. This is practically 75 per cent destroyed. Balance is now operating . . . also trying to rebuild the damaged parts. Must admit that the flyers that have attacked plant did a very good job . . . At both Annendorf and Halle they are installing smoke-screen devices. They are very small and look about as follows (sketch attached). They are located 150 metres apart and surround the entire plant . . .

'Sigmaringen—home of the Vichy Government. Laval and Pétain both alive in the castle of Count Hohenzollern (who is imprisoned under suspicion that he had something to do with 20 July). Laval has his office and the rest of the Government officials in a schoolhouse close by. Happened to see him incidentally. The Vichy Government is training and equipping a French army there.

'Berchesgrend—the place is apparently not to be found on any map, since the place is a new suburb between Berlin and Juterborg. The plant is manufacturing the new turbines for the new plane (jet). The new motors are made by the new Ganheim company. Plant is located on the right-hand side of the tracks from Berlin to Juterborg. It is a tremendous plant and is well concealed in the woods. Around the plant there is a double wire fence about 2.5 metres. About 8000 workers in three shifts. The new plane has no propeller. Speed 720 km. Witnessed trial flights at both Ludwigshafen and Friedrichshafen (See my separate reports on those— map attached) . . .'

It was a tremendous piece of industrial intelligence and was to help the 8th's Flying Fortresses put one of its greatest enemies over Germany out of action—the jet ME 262s. But Erickson, in his hotel room, was no longer concerned with his mission; he knew now that every additional minute he spent in Germany could well hasten his arrest by the Gestapo. Still his allotted time in Germany had not run out; neither did he have the necessary permission to leave the country.

In despair he sent the agreed telegram to Prince Carl. It read, 'Returning in three or four days. Handle the scheduled luncheon conference in my place. But make no commitments until I return. Erickson.'

Carl Bernadotte knew what to do.

Just as Erickson had about decided to 'go underground' and try to smuggle himself out of Germany, he received the long awaited telegram from Sweden. It said: 'Bad news. Your wife is very ill. Imperative you return instantly to her bedside. Dr Gunnar Petersen.'

Aware that all foreign telegrams were censored by the Gestapo, but unaware that Schellenberg was already sounding out Count Bernadotte as to whether he would play the role of intermediary between the *Reichsführer* and the Western Allies, Erickson telephoned the Gestapo HQ and asked for permission to board the next plane to Stockholm.

It was granted almost immediately and the next day he left Tempelhof Field for the last time, his mission accomplished.

Erickson and Prince Carl spent the remaining months of the war in Sweden, the objects of increasing suspicion and dislike in a country which was now definitely anti-Nazi. Finally, on 3 June, the American Embassy in Stockholm decided to make a public declaration of the real role the two men had played during the war. That morning the *New York Times* carried a feature story captioned: 'SWEDISH "PRO-NAZI" DUPED FOR 3 YEARS: BLACKLISTED BY US, HE SENT ALLIES SECRET DATA ON SYNTHETIC GASOLINE PLANTS.'

Erickson was vindicated at last.[3]

---

[3] There are still some in Sweden, however, who do not accept this version. Both Erickson and the Prince remain controversial figures.

3

COLONEL GISKES MAKES AN APPEARANCE

While Allen Dulles and Colonel David Bruce, the two senior OSS men in Europe, were busy trying to infiltrate Germany in order to help the US Army's advance which had now apparently bogged down in the Ardennes-Eifel area, their chief back in Washington was considering whether the elimination of Hitler might not be the best means of bringing the whole business to an immediate end.

Learning that Hitler and Mussolini might meet in the Brenner area, which was clearly becoming a centre of concentration for their combined forces, the representatives of SO [OSS's Subversive Operations] suggested at a top level meeting: 'Let us parachute a cadre of our toughest men into the area and shoot up the bastards! Sure, it'll be a suicide operation but that's what we're organized to carry out.'

General Donovan turned to Dr Lovell: 'How would Professor Moriarty capitalize on this situation?' he asked.

Lovell said, 'I propose an attack which they cannot anticipate. They'll meet in the conference room of an inn or a hotel. If we can have one operator for five minutes or less in that room, just before they gather there, that is really all we need.'

There was some scepticism among his colleagues, but Lovell went on to explain: 'I suggest that he brings a vase filled with cut flowers in water and that he places it on the conference table or nearby ... In this janitor's hand is a capsule containing liquid nitrogen-mustard gas. It's a new chemical derivative which has no odour whatever, is colourless and floats on water. I have it available at my laboratory ... As our man places the bouquet on the conference table, he crushes the capsule and drops it in among the flowers. An invisible, oily film spreads over the water in the dish and starts vaporizing. Our man is safely out and I think he should disappear into Switzerland if possible.'

'What happens to the men at the conference?' asked Donovan.

'Well, if they are in that room for twenty minutes, the invisible gas will have the peculiar property of affecting their bodies through the naked eyeballs. Everyone in that room will be permanently blinded. The optic nerve will be atrophied and never function again. A blind leader can't continue the war—at least I don't believe he can.'

As Lovell had anticipated, the suggestion aroused a great deal of excited controversy, but he was not finished yet. 'There's a big pay-off possible, if it is done. Let's be completely bold in capitalizing on the event. If the Pope would issue a Papal Bull or whatever is appropriate, it might read something like this: "My children, God in his infinite wisdom has stricken your leaders blind. His sixth Commandment is Thou Shalt Not Kill. This blindness of your leaders is a warning that you should lay down your arms and return to the ways of peace."'

Turning to Donovan, who was a strict Catholic, Lovell said: 'General, this may appear to be a suggestion of hypocrisy that the Pope is asked to practise, but a great number of the German and Italian fighting forces are Roman Catholics. They will heed Pius XII. If he can use his high office to stop this killing, isn't he advancing the cause of Christianity more than any man on earth?'

Donovan promised that he would discuss the suggestion with a friend of his who was a member of the United States Catholic hierarchy [probably Cardinal Spellman], but nothing came of it. Hitler and Mussolini met elsewhere, changing their meeting place at the last moment as the Führer often did.[1]

But in that winter of 1944, while the Allied Armies in Western Europe 'regrouped', as Montgomery was fond of

---

[1] Hitler often maintained that anyone could kill him easily; the only way to protect his life was to announce an appearance at a particular place at a particular time and then, at the last moment, change both the place and the time.

180

calling the stalemate, prior to launching the death blow at the body of the Reich, the OSS planners, safely ensconced in their air-conditioned Washington offices, could not stop putting forward hare-brained schemes for getting rid of the Führer.

Undismayed by the failure of his plan to assassinate Hitler with poison gas, Dr Lovell looked into the possibility of attacking him through his glands. Top American diagnosticians agreed with Lovell that Hitler's 'poor emotional control, his violent passions, his selection of companions like Roehm' indicated that the Führer was on the borderline between male and female. Lovell felt that it might be possible to nudge him to the female side in the hope that 'his moustache would fall off and his voice become soprano'.

His plan envisaged smuggling a gardener into his entourage who would doctor the home-grown vegetables for his personal table with female sex hormones. These would upset Hitler's whole hormonal balance and radically affect his direction of the war. The scheme was approved by Donovan, but Lovell heard no more of it. As he wrote in his account of his backroom operations, *Of Spies & Stratagems*: 'Since he [Hitler] survived, I can only assume that the gardener took our money and threw the syringes and medications into the nearest thicket. Either that or Hitler had a big turnover in "tasters".'

But in the middle of that strange limbo on the Western Front which took place between October and December, 1944, the OSS planners were not alone in their capacity for dreaming up weird and wonderful plans for clandestine operations into the heart of Twelveland.

In London, too, the SOE, SIS's heartily disliked rival, also discussed some hare-brained schemes. Its German section[2] had begun toying with a raid on the Führer's HQ in early autumn, inspired by the success of Skorzeny's daring rescue of Mussolini from the top of the Gran Sasso the previous September.

Six years earlier Colonel MacFarlane, a former Intelligence officer and then military attaché in Berlin, had

[2] Amazingly enough the SIS did not have a 'German' section throughout the war!

planned to assassinate Hitler. In great detail he worked out a scheme to shoot Hitler as he took the salute at a parade in Berlin, firing at him from the balcony of his Charlottenburg Chaussee flat. At a range of 100 yards and using a silenced rifle, equipped with a telescopic sight, MacFarlane hoped that the roar of the crowd would drown any sound and his position on the British diplomatic staff shield him from any suspicion. He put the plan forward to the Government of the day, but it was vetoed because, as MacFarlane told his daughter in disgust, 'They said that it was unsportsmanlike!'[3]

By 1944 the powers-that-be no longer thought it 'unsportsmanlike'. Captured German generals were carefully quizzed to find out details of Hitler's headquarters; a plan was drawn up of the FHQ's security arrangements and detailed biographical sketches made of Hitler's private court, including one of his then hardly-known mistress, Eva Braun.

Then, after considerable research work had been done, the whole scheme was abandoned as suddenly as it had begun. But the new head of the SOE's German Section, General Templer, who had been in Intelligence himself at the beginning of the war before he had been posted to the Middle East, where unfortunately his fighting career came to an abrupt halt when a looted piano fell off a truck travelling in front of him and broke his back, was full of enthusiasm for operations into the heart of Twelveland.

One of the schemes originated under his command was to drop carrier pigeons over Germany with little questionnaires about troop movements attached to their legs. Any German who hated the régime and wanted to bring about its end could then forward the intelligence to the SOE in London without any risk to himself.

Sefton Delmer, the ex-chief reporter of the *Daily Express*, who was in charge of 'black radio' operations[4] to Germany

---

[3] By a remarkable coincidence, *Life* published a fictionalized account of an attempt to murder Hitler, and Geoffrey Household wrote his famous thriller *Rogue Male*, a thinly fictionalized story of a murder attempt on the Führer at the same time as MacFarlane was planning the real thing. Was there any significance in the fact that Household was also an SIS agent?

[4] Primarily *Soldatensender Calais*, beamed at the German Forces from within Europe.

and was present, then suggested a variation to the proved technique that had brought in a great deal of intelligence from the former occupied countries. He told Templer, 'That's a splendid idea. I suggest that in addition to parachuting live birds with questionnaires in their boxes we should also drop dead ones without boxes but with questionnaires attached to their legs, which have already been completed—by ourselves.'

Templer roared with laughter at the scheme and approved it immediately, for he saw at once what it would lead to—a massive Gestapo search for 'traitors'. He laughed even more when Delmer, who had spent his youth in Berlin and was well acquainted with the German mentality, suggested that the questionnaires should be filled in in such a manner that the Gestapo would suspect they had come from Party members trying to ingratiate themselves with the victorious Allies. The pigeons were duly dropped and quite a number of answered questionnaires were received from Germans who found the live ones; but there was no reaction on the dead ones.

One day, however, a tired pigeon flew into the SOE London lofts with a polite message scrawled over the questionnaire, reading: '*I had the sister of this one for supper. Delicious! Please send us some more!*'

Thus the Intelligence men spent the early winter of 1944, apparently unconcerned by the absolute dearth of information coming out of the Reich, unaware that an old enemy had returned to the scene of his earliest counter-espionage triumphs—Herman Giskes, now Colonel Giskes, commander of the 4th Front Reconnaissance Section (*Frontaufklaerungskommando*), located at Dersdorf near Bonn.

Giskes had played a tremendous counter-intelligence role throughout the war, running the infamous 'North Pole' operation in Holland during 1942–1944, using 'turned' Dutch SOE operatives to capture forty-two of their comrades parachuted into Holland. In the summer of 1944 he had been posted to Paris and just before he left had succeeded in marrying off one of his agents, a descendant of a famous Australian military family working for the German war industry in Paris, to Jacqueline de Broglie. But Jacqueline was no ordinary member of the Parisian 'jet set' of that time. Educated at Heathfield School and brought up at Donnington Hall, she was a scion of the Singer sewing machine family and related to Churchill himself. Thus, when Paris was liberated in the summer of 1944 and she returned to England, her husband 'Freddy' followed her two months later in the uniform of a captain in the British Army. 'He wasn't blackmailed into doing so,' Giskes said.[5] 'He volunteered to do so and even worked out the way we should communicate after he arrived in London himself.' Thus, just before the *Abwehr* was broken up and Giskes given command of one of its surviving units, he pulled off the great coup of infiltrating an agent right into the Churchill family itself.[6]

Now, in early November, he was summoned from his headquarters to drive through the Eifel to Field-Marshal Model's HQ at Bad Muenstereifel. There he and another former *Abwehr* officer were interviewed by Model's Chief-of-Intelligence and asked if they could think of any scheme which would use Allied nationals to fool the Western Allies about the Model Army Group's strategic intentions. The other man said straightaway that it would be impossible at this stage of the war to get Allied nationals to work for the Germans. Giskes asked for four hours to think about it.

After enjoying an 'excellent dinner' at the HQ, he outlined his plan to the Chief-of-Intelligence and then asked if he could not be told exactly what the Army's target really was. Model's staff officer replied that that was strictly forbidden and he, Giskes, would have to take his word for it that a great new operation in the West was already well beyond the planning stage and would shake the enemy out of their self-satisfied complacency.

The result of that somewhat puzzling meeting with Model's Chief-of-Intelligence was *Operation Heinrich*, executed by a Giskes who did not know what really lay

[5] In a conversation with the author.
[6] There is some doubt as to what happened to 'Freddy'. Both Morrison and Miss Ellen Wilkinson, Parliamentary Under-Secretary, were questioned on the subject in the House of Commons in 1945. In the end Morrison stated that the 'Spy in the Churchill family' is still alive in Austria today.

behind it till the very last moment, with men who thought they were aiding the Allied cause but who, in reality, were German dupes.

Recruiting a German engineer in a border labour camp employing French and Belgian labour who got on well with the forced labourers, Giskes told him he wanted to help some of the men to escape. The engineer was horrified until Giskes explained that the escapees would, in fact, be helping the German cause. In the end the engineer agreed, and approaching the selected escapees, explained that he was really a communist and would like them to escape to carry messages for him to the first American officer they met after they had crossed the front line.

Once they had obtained the forced labourers' co-operation, Giskes dreamed up his own German 'offensive'—a two pronged attack on Aachen[7]—and supplied them with rough-and-ready 'secret' details, which were written down on scraps of paper in milk and hidden about their persons. If the Americans wanted more information they should include the words 'Regards to Otto from Saxony' [the supposed communist engineer] in the daily German news broadcast from Allied-controlled Radio Luxembourg.

Ten days after the first labourer had 'escaped', it gave Giskes a certain amount of sardonic pleasure to hear the Luxembourg announcer on the other side of the border announce in his unmistakable local accent, 'And tonight we send regards to Otto from Saxony!'

Thereafter Giskes managed to smuggle ten 'escapees' through the front, each of them carrying a new piece of information from the communist 'Otto from Saxony' which indicated that the 'enemy' would launch a spoiling attack against American-held Aachen. On 16 December, 1944, the massive bombardment which began at 5.45 a.m. on the 'ghost front', to be followed by an attack launched by three German armies, totalling half a million men, revealed to General Sibert, Bradley's head of Intelligence in Luxembourg City, just how badly he had been fooled.

While the OSS and SOE had been toying with their

[7] Giskes was worried at first that the Aachen thrust might well be the real direction of the German offensive. He need not have feared.

incredible schemes to bring the war to a speedy end, their men in the field had suffered an incredible defeat. And what of the 'professionals'—the Secret Intelligence Service? Why hadn't their agents in Twelveland reported anything? Hadn't the 'Shadow OKW' been able to pinpoint the coming attack on the basis of the information supplied to it by Bletchley?

Why was it that the two surviving copies of the highly classified 'Top Secret' intelligence digests, which Eisenhower's Supreme Headquarters prepared regularly for distribution to its subordinate army groups, were destroyed after the war 'for security reasons', as General Sir Kenneth Strong, Eisenhower's Chief-of-Intelligence maintains?[8]

A lot of questions and very few satisfactory answers. But America's 'European Pearl Harbor' made America's spymasters swear that there would not be another intelligence failure in Europe. From now on the Intelligence war with Twelveland would be fought with that kind of harsh bitterness that only Americans can achieve when they feel their innocence and inherent goodness have been betrayed.

---

[8] The 'Top Secrets' contained the latest and most up to date operational intelligence and were distributed in a special cypher. They were usually destroyed by their high-ranking recipients after use. Two copies were kept, however: one at Supreme Headquarters and one in London. Both these were destroyed.

PART FOUR

DROP INTO THE REDOUBT

(1944–45)

'An intelligence service is the ideal vehicle for a conspiracy. Its members can travel about at home and abroad under secret orders and no questions asked.'

Allen Dulles on the
German Intelligence Services.

1

OPERATION GREEN-UP BEGINS

One afternoon early in January, 1945, the telephone rang in the SD headquarters for the province of Tyrol-Vorarlberg in Innsbruck. *Hauptsturmfuehrer* Wandel, in charge of the SD's wireless listening station at Bregenz on Lake Constance, was on the 'phone. He wanted to speak to the head of the Innsbruck office, *Sturmbannfuehrer* Gontard. 'What's going on up there?' he asked. 'You building an alpine fortification system or something?'

Gontard's reply was to ask his subordinate whether he had been drinking. Wandel replied that he had never been so serious. 'We've just picked up a message from Dulles to Washington stating that we Germans are building a tremendous fortification system in the Alps.'

Gontard listened to Wandel's excited account of the planned German defensive system, which would include all the mountainous area of northern Italy, Austria and southern Germany, with growing disbelief. In the end he hung up on Wandel, telling him he would report the matter to *Gauleiter* Hofer, who had his command post at Bolzano in South Tyrol.

At this time the *Gauleiter* was the uncrowned king of most of Austria and the former Italian Tyrol with its predominantly German-speaking population. When Italy had gone over to the Allies in late 1943, not only had he incorporated the Italian provinces of Bolzano, Trentino and Belluno into his own *Gau* and banned the Italian fascist party, but had also forbidden the National Socialist Overseas Organization, run by Bradford-born Ernst Bohle. Thus when Gontard was received by the *Gauleiter* in his Command Post, situated at the local Marcellina Monastery, he knew that Hofer was not a man who tolerated fools gladly. He reported what Wandel had told him and then waited for the storm. It did not come.

Slowly Hofer turned his massive head towards him and began to laugh, while Gontard watched him in astonishment. Finally the *Gauleiter* pulled himself together and said, 'Gontard, that is the best idea that the Americans have had in this war. That Alpine fortification business is going to be our salvation.'

Thus the great deception was born.

When the Ardennes counter-offensive burst on the surprised US Army, the OSS had had exactly four men inside Germany. Not one of them had any kind of communication with either London or Paris and they were producing no intelligence whatsoever. Frantically the OSS launched a crash operation to infiltrate agents into Germany, recruiting them mostly from the OSS Labor Branch's German section run by Arthur Goldberg in London, and from the ranks of the International Transport Workers' Federation, led by the Belgian unionist Omer Becu. Scores of agents were hurriedly smuggled through the confused Ardennes front with disastrous results; casualties were terribly high.[1]

As an emergency measure a wealthy 32-year-old New York tax-lawyer named William Casey was appointed to co-ordinate all operations within Germany. Speedily he re-organized the various agencies sending agents into the Reich and tried to give a new sense of security to the brave if amateurish volunteers from Poland, Belgium and France who were to risk their necks in enemy territory. From the end of January when the Ardennes offensive was finally beaten, he started dispatching them into the Reich. Those intended for duties close to the major crossroad cities in the Rhineland were smuggled through the front in the Eifel

---

[1] In the Belgian border village in which I live, the old people recollect one such agent who appeared three times there during the German occupation, wearing German officer's uniform, in order to direct operations against the main German front. After the village had been liberated in January, 1945, he appeared again, this time in US uniform. One of his comrades, Code-named 'Armand' was not so fortunate. Crossing the St Vith–Malmédy road, some four miles from my village, he was caught and shot out of hand. His grave is still there.

by the US Army; the remainder, intended for deeper penetration, were flown in from Dijon in France or Namur in Belgium.

By early March, when Patton's Third Army was beginning its march to the Rhine, Casey had some 150 agents within Germany with some as far afield as Berlin, Munich and Regensburg.

Regensburg had been picked as their centre of operations by two Belgian agents, who bore the code-name *Chauffeur*. Dropped on 31 March, they had the rare good luck to discover a local dairy, run by forced labour from Belgian and French POW camps. The POWs agreed to help them immediately and they were able to set up their transmitter in the dairy's silo. It was the OSS's first-ever permanent transmitter in the Reich.

They also started using the dairy milk trucks to move around the surrounding countryside. And their luck continued to hold. When one of the agents discovered a French girl working in a Regensburg brothel, not only did she satisfy his sexual needs but she also agreed to spy on her German military customers. Thus it was that the Belgian squatted in a cupboard in the prostitute's room, taking notes of her customers' indiscreet comments. It must have been a weird experience, though it is hardly reflected in the laconic style of the report resulting from it: 'The German General Staff is at Regensburg, Hotel du Parc, Maximilianstrasse, the street facing the station, first house on the left.'

Another OSS team, code-named 'Hammer', even managed to penetrate the German capital itself. Two Czechs, who had been equipped with papers identifying them as toolmakers fleeing from the Russians, parachuted blind into Germany on the night of 2 March, 1945. Landing in a meadow not far from Alt Friesack, some thirty miles west of Berlin, they walked to the nearest railway station and took a train into the capital. There they took refuge with the parents of one of the agents and employed the agent's sister and brother-in-law to obtain military information for them. Once, when one of the Czechs was returning home, he was stopped by an SS patrol. The troopers found his papers in order, but wanted to search his briefcase which was full of incriminating papers. But the Czech toolmaker was up to the situation; first he opened a pillowslip filled with dirty laundry which he always carried with him. The SS man rumpled up his nose and let the Czech agent pass, which probably saved his life, for the toolmaker had already cocked his pistol and was ready to shoot it out if the Germans discovered the secret papers.

Although the Czechs were not equipped with a transmitter, they did have the J–E equipment and on the night of 28 March, they successfully contacted a Mosquito flying 20,000 feet above the outskirts of the capital; as the J–E operator wrote later in his dispatch to London: 'Hammer stated that the Klingenberg power plant on Rommelsberg Lake was fully functioning and was furnishing electric power to factories . . . He added: "We need medicine that soldiers can take in order to become ill, four pistols and three knives, also food stamps or paper on which stamps can be forged. Please give our regards to our wives and children".'[2]

But Dulles, in Berne, was not particularly impressed by the OSS agents' reports on the conditions pertaining in Berlin and the goings-on of the German soldiery in Regensburg's brothels. He was more concerned with German strategy once the Allies had crossed the Rhine. Would they fight on or would they surrender? He was inclined to believe the former. But how and where?

Dulles knew that in the early 'forties the Swiss had constructed their 'National Redoubt', a mountain fortification system in which they would fight if they were attacked by the Germans. The kind of terrain into which the Germans were being pushed by the Allies was exactly the same as that in which the Swiss had built their own 'redoubt'. As more and more unconfirmed reports came into Berne that the major Nazi leaders such as Bormann were evacuating their families into that area and that several important Nazis themselves had been seen there, Dulles began to conclude that the Germans were going to imitate the Swiss. No single piece of information could be confirmed, but Dulles started

[2] On 24 April, the Red Army pushed forward to find the Hammer team fighting to prevent the *Wehrmacht* from blowing up a bridge. They were evacuated to London.

reporting to Washington his suspicion that the Germans were building a vast 'National Redoubt' in the Alps.

His fears were increased when the Austrian 'resistance' movement '05' reported that Hofer had been to the Führer's HQ to discuss the fortification with Hitler himself.[3] Alarmed that Hofer was intending to turn Southern Germany and Austria into a battlefield, they contacted the OSS in Switzerland and relayed their fears to them. In his turn, Dulles passed them on to Washington.

By early March, 1945, these views were reflected by Eisenhower's change in strategy, which ordered that the main direction of the Allied push would not be against Berlin but against the 'Redoubt'; for as the SHAEF Intelligence summary for 11 March had it:

'Here, defended by nature and by the most efficient secret weapons yet invented, the powers that have hitherto guided Germany will survive to reorganize her resurrection; here armaments will be manufactured in bomb-proof factories, food and equipment will be stored in vast underground caverns and a specially selected corps of young men will be trained in guerrilla warfare so that a whole underground army can be fitted and directed to liberate Germany from the occupying forces.'[4]

As William L. Shirer observed in his *Rise and Fall of the Third Reich*, 'It would almost seem as though the Allied Supreme Commander's intelligence staff had been infiltrated by British and American mystery writers!'

But it was an appreciation that was taken seriously by both Eisenhower's Chief-of-Staff, Bedell Smith, who expressed his concern to journalists that there might be 'a prolonged campaign in the Alpine area', and Allen Dulles in Berne, the unwitting father of the whole deception. Thus it was that he ordered 'Operation Green-Up' to begin. Its terms of reference were: the reconnaissance of the 'Alpine

[3] Hofer did suggest some form of fortification at the meeting, but Hitler vetoed it. Goebbels, however, picked up the idea and used his propaganda media to try to convince the Allies that an 'Alpine Redoubt' really was being built.

[4] This reference is to the German *Werewolf* movement. For further details. see the author's *Werewolf* (Leo Cooper, 1972).

Fortress'; sabotage of the area's most important defence installations and establishing of contacts with the Austrian 'resistance' movement.

Operation Green-Up was composed of a three-man OSS team. Its leader was German-born OSS sergeant Fred Mayer, a former paratrooper who had volunteered for the organization. Mayer was twenty-five, well-built and athletic. With him was a Dutch radio operator, Hans Boysen, aged twenty-three, and an Austrian, Aloys Martin, aged twenty-five who had climbed many of the Tyrol's peaks.

On an icy cold night in March the three left their base in Bari and were dropped over the Stubaier Alps in West Austria by a Liberator bomber. The drop was successful save that two pairs of skis which were dropped separately were lost. While his two companions floundered through the deep snow, Mayer skiid ahead, dragging their equipment behind him on a sledge until he reached a ski hut, where they spent the night.

The next morning the three of them, dressed in German *Wehrmacht* uniforms, reported to the burgomaster in the neighbouring village of Gries. They explained to him that they were members of a German alpine unit who had been separated from their comrades and asked if he could help them to get to Innsbruck. He obliged and the same evening they were established among friends in Oberpfuss, a suburb of the city.

There 'Green-Up' went into operation almost at once. Boysen contacted Bari and was rewarded by an acknowledgement from the BBC, which often ran messages for agents in its evening programmes. 'Attention Alice Moll! Cherry blossoms from Tokyo have arrived.'[5]

Thereafter Mayer signalled the arrival of Mussolini and the former French premier in the 'Redoubt', as well as the establishment of Himmler's headquarters there—all indications to Dulles that the Germans meant business in the Tyrol. He also reported that the Germans had been timing the Italian-based 15th USAAF Air Force's bombing of the Brenner Pass and were running their rail schedule accordingly. Soon thereafter the Air Force changed the timing of

[5] Alice Moll was a former girlfriend of Mayer's

7. Commander Alexander Denniston—the picture is from his passport issued in 1938, in which he is described as a 'Civil Servant'.

8. Kim Philby at a press conference held in 1955 because of his rumoured connection with the Burgess and Maclean case.

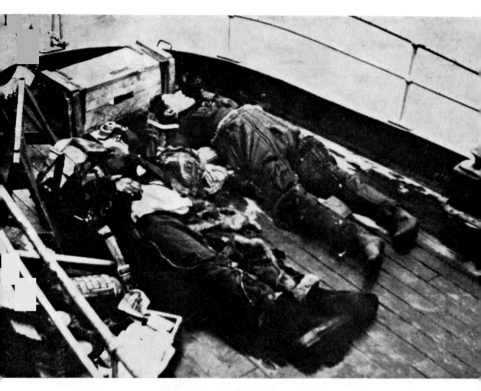

9. The bodies of the crew of the plane which crashed over Gibraltar in 1943 killing General Sikorski, premier of the Polish Government in exile.

10. Admiral Canaris shortly before his arrest.

11. A photograph of Frederick Winterbotham taken on the publication of his book *The Ultra Secret* in 1974.

their attacks and managed to block the pass for days on end.

But time was running out for Mayer. A week after his arrival in Innsbruck he obtained a German *Oberleutnant*'s uniform and papers from the local 'resistance' and continued his espionage activities in this guise until, thinking that he was becoming known in the city, he dreamed up another cover—that of a French worker who had been employed in Wiener-Neustadt as an electrician before being forced to flee before the advancing Russians. Returning from a reconnaissance mission to the local Messerschmitt works in this disguise, he saw the blue sweater hanging out of his girlfriend's window which indictated the coast was clear. Without a second thought he entered the house to be captured by two German MPs armed with sub-machine guns.

Mayer tried to bluster it out, sticking to his cover story (he spoke excellent French). What he did not know was that one of the Austrian 'resisters', a black-marketeer, had betrayed him to the enemy.

That night he was taken through Innsbruck's blacked-out streets to the local Gestapo HQ. There Senior Inspector Busch began the 'special questioning'. When Mayer refused to answer, Busch passed him over to three SD men under the command of a bull-like Munich *Kriminalsekretaer* named Walter Guettner. There the questioning became even more 'special'. Mayer, realizing what he was in for, tried to swallow his poison capsule. In vain; the 'special questioning' went on.

For over four hours they beat him, 'making a pulp' of his face and bursting an eardrum. Mayer stuck to his cover until he was confronted by the traitor; then he admitted he was an OSS man, but refused to betray his two companions. Guettner went to work on him with redoubled energy. He was doubled over an iron bar, which was placed between his tied arms and knees. Hung upside down thus, water was forced into his nostrils and damaged ear until he blacked out.

After six hours of torture the police dragged him, half conscious, back to Oberpfuss and began a house-to-house search for his accomplices. But they had been warned and fled to a secret hideout. The torture began all over again. A punch in the face knocked out four of his teeth. Another

195

smashed his nose and with each blow his three torturers bellowed in unison: 'Where is the radio operator?'

Then fate took a hand. The door opened to reveal Inspector Busch and the Nazi *Kreisleiter*[6] for Innsbruck, Dr Max Primbs. Busch asked: 'How are you getting on?'

Guettner shook his head. 'He'll let himself be beaten to death before he admits anything.'

Primbs said: 'Stop beating him. If this man is an OSS agent, I must report the fact to the *Gauleiter*. It is much more important than you think'.

[6] Roughly 'senior leader'.

2

CONFUSION IN THE REDOUBT

Gauleiter Hofer was waiting for Mayer at his home in the *Lachhof* overlooking Innsbruck. In his eagerness to find out what the US agent was up to, he did not seem to notice the state of Mayer's face. Neither, apparently, did Mayer. Introducing himself as 'First Lieutenant' Mayer to impress the Germans, he said boldly that he would be ready to negotiate between Hofer and the Allies if he were prepared to surrender Innsbruck, the 'capital' of the Alpine Redoubt.

Hofer was not prepared for such a bold approach. But Mayer's confidence strengthened his own conviction that he must not make a wrong move at this crucial stage in the war. He knew already that Dulles was secretly discussing surrender terms for the German forces in Italy with SS General Wolff, once Himmler's representative at Hitler's HQ.

Indeed, at that very moment (unknown to Hofer), a young OSS agent was being hidden in Wolff's HQ at nearby Bolzano in order to maintain communications between the SS General and Dulles in Switzerland. He was a young Czech named 'Wally' who had escaped from Dachau Concentration Camp and volunteered to work as a radio-operator for the OSS.

Twice he had just escaped arrest and on the day that Mayer had been betrayed, his 'hosts' had been forced to lock him in a linen cupboard because American bombers had dropped their load on Bolzano and killed several staff officers. He had heard angry voices in the corridor outside and an enraged staff officer had hammered on the door of his hiding place. If the USAF bombed the place again, he was warned, he would be shot without trial. That evening, at about the time Mayer was received by Hofer, Wally radioed his bosses that if a bomb landed only fifty metres from Wolff's HQ, he would be taken out and shot. '*Wally ist verloren*',[1] he closed his message plaintively, speaking of himself in the third person, as if he were already dead.

Hofer knew all this. But he knew, too, that if the surrender were to have any strategic significance for the Allies it must include the German Army in the Alpine Redoubt and it was his intention to make Dulles pay for that: Hofer was to be left in charge and, after the Allied troops had passed through, west Austria would not be occupied by them.

For a while he sounded Mayer out, but before they got down to detailed discussion Inspector Busch appeared. Fearful for his own safety, Busch protested against the high-handed manner with which Mayer had been removed from the Gestapo prison in the Herrengasse. What if Kaltenbrunner,[2] who was now in the area, found out. 'I'll hang from the nearest tree,' he said plaintively. Hofer agreed that something had to be done and suggested that Mayer should be imprisoned in Lager Reichenau near Innsbruck, where he had a better chance of surviving than in the Gestapo prison.

Although Guettner protested when Busch told him, he was too busy preparing his own escape from Innsbruck to take the matter further. As a result Mayer, who still thought he was going to be executed, was taken to the camp. And there, for the time being, the matter rested while Hofer studied developments in the confused situation within the Redoubt, taking great care that the military commander, Field-Marshal Kesselring, and the head of the Reich's Main Security Office, Kaltenbrunner, who like himself was an Austrian, still regarded him as a loyal follower of the Führer. But he need not have worried about Kaltenbrunner, for he had already made his own contacts with a member of

[1] Wally is lost.
[2] Ernst Kaltenbrunner had taken over as head of the Reich's Main Security Office.

an Allied secret service, the SOE's mysterious 'Major George'.

The men who had run that tremendous counter-intelligence and police *apparat*, which had been Heydrich's fatal bequest to the German nation, had begun to flee Berlin and sneak into the Alpine Redoubt in April, 1945. In the course of that month, they all deserted their posts—Kaltenbrunner, Gestapo Mueller, Skorzeny, Eichmann—and, perhaps believing their own lies, taken refuge in the mountains. Kaltenbrunner, assuming the identity of an Army captain, had set up his headquarters in a renovated stable close to the village of Altaussee in the Salzkammergut. There, with his 21-year-old mistress, Gisela von Westarp, who had been Himmler's secretary before she had given birth to Kaltenbrunner's twins, he waited.

When the head of the SDs counter-intelligence organization in South-East Europe, *Obersturmbannführer* Hoettl, informed Kaltenbrunner that there was a British-led Austrian partisan group in the Aussee area, Kaltenbrunner decided to contact them. He felt, like Hoettl, who was also an Austrian, that the British would like to see a non-communist government established in eastern Austria in opposition to the communist-dominated one already set up in the Russian-occupied zone. Accordingly he ordered Hoettl to contact 'Major George' of the SOE, who Hoettl knew had his headquarters at the small town of Eselbach.

Thus the SS Colonel met 'Major George', who eight months before had been a corporal in the German Army, to discuss the formation of a new Austrian government.

Major George's real name was Albrecht Gaiswinkler. Born in Altaussee, where he had worked in the local hospital before being called up, he had deserted in France in August, 1944. There he had volunteered to join the SOE and to parachute into Austria with a group of fellow Austrians. Soon the little group had established a partisan formation which had since carried out extensive espionage operations throughout that part of Austria.

Major George was not impressed by Hoettl's story that he was really working for the American Counter-Intelligence Corps and that his major concern was the speedy establishment of a free and western-orientated Austria. However, he said he would support Kaltenbrunner's attempts to establish a government and radio his superiors the list of 'ministers' proposed. He had one condition however:

'Hitler has had art treasures from throughout Europe hidden in the Aussee salt mines. *Gauleiter* Eigruber is going to blow them up. He's had six large crates transported to the mine. They're labelled "Marble. Do not drop!" But in reality they contain the explosives for the job—US air mines. Not only will they destroy the art treasures but they'll put most of the local people around here out of work if the mine is blocked by the explosion.'

Hoettl agreed to persuade Kaltenbrunner to have the explosives taken from the mine and sunk in the Aussee. When Eigruber heard what Kaltenbrunner had done, he decided to raise the explosives from the lake. Eigruber also managed to convince the C.O. of a tank unit equipped with mobile flame-throwers to move into the area. His orders were to enter the mine and burn the works of art the following morning.

When Major George heard that the Kaltenbrunner plan had failed, he ordered his partisans into operation. His men stole Teller mines during the night from a local German engineer battalion. With them they blew up the entrance to the mine just before the tank company made its appearance, leaving only two minute entrances free (air shafts known only to Major George's men).

The infuriated tank C.O. ordered his men to start clearing the main entrance and Major George knew that he could not possibly stop the soldiers with his partisans. So he sent couriers to fetch help from the US 80th Division, which had reached Traunsee. The commanding general was finally convinced that the couriers were genuine and sent a combat team under the command of a Major Pearson to tackle the German tank company.

With Major George's help, Major Pearson broke through the German line, kidnapped General Fabiunke of the German VI Army off the street in Bad Aussee and persuaded him to surrender his troops. Finally Pearson got through to the mine to find that the German soldiers had withdrawn thirty minutes before. Later an Allied commission estimated the value of the treasures contained in the mine to be the equivalent of fourteen million marks!

But in the course of his 36-hour dash to save the works of art, Pearson narrowly missed capturing an elderly German in the uniform of a second-lieutenant in the *Wehrmacht*.

Major George's men had spotted him before he disappeared on his journey south, which in years to come was to cost the intelligence services of half-a-dozen countries so much money and time. They thought it odd that the over-age lieutenant gave orders to his two companions, both high-ranking officers of the SS, and was obeyed. But they had other things on their mind and did nothing about it. By the time they came to reflect on the matter the lieutenant was gone.

For the lieutenant was that same 'decent little man' who had questioned Stevens and Best in the cellars of Number 8, Prinz Albrecht Strasse so long before and who had sent the latter cigarettes during his long stay in Sachsenhausen Concentration Camp. He was none other than the head of that infamous organization which had held Europe in terror these last six years—Gestapo Mueller![3]

[3] Most of his colleagues were captured soon afterwards. One by one the men who had run the Reich's Main Security Office were taken prisoner and sentenced. Kaltenbrunner was betrayed inadvertently by his young mistress and executed at Nuremburg. Mueller was assumed dead in Berlin in 1945 but when his grave was dug up in 1965, it was found to contain the bones of *three much younger men.*

3

SERGEANT MAYER CAPTURES THE CAPITAL

While Sergeant Mayer waited to see what the Nazi *Gauleiter* would do, Gestapo Mueller's two most important intelligence prisoners moved into the Reichenau Camp where he was being held.

After five and a half years' imprisonment in Sachsenhausen Concentration Camp the two heads of the Continental Secret Service were on the move again. They had spent the last week in Floessenburg Concentration Camp where they had witnessed the death of Admiral Canaris. Naked, his nose broken, he had been garrotted by a chicken wire for his supposed part in the July plot to kill Hitler. Thereafter his body had been cremated, the wind blowing the ashes throughout the camp. Now they were in Reichenau, together with the rest of the *Prominenten*, waiting for shipment to an unknown destination.[1]

But in spite of his five and a half years in jail, Best, the former chief of the 'Z' Organization, still remained the standard Continental caricature of an Englishman: very skinny, dressed in a check jacket and flannel trousers and wearing a monocle, 'always showing his big false horse's teeth in an obliging smile,' as one of his German fellow prisoners wrote, 'and displaying that trustworthy discretion which engenders deepest confidence'.

But, Best felt 'unsettled and nervy, wondering what had been happening at the front and what the immediate future held for us'. He spent most of the day wandering around the camp in the hot spring sun, followed by a prisoner carrying

[1] They included a General Halder who had complained so bitterly about the betrayal of German General Staff secrets, as well as several SIS and SOE agents.

his precious suitcase: as an officer and a gentleman, he had always insisted that he could not carry it himself, and the Germans had obliged him with a prisoner to do it for him.

He didn't like what he saw: the lavatories 'open cesspools'; the American prisoners 'more like skeletons than living men'; and bugs everywhere. Fortunately, however, he did not have to stay long at Reichenau. One of his fellow prisoners, a German canon, managed to get one of the guards to buy a parcel of food in Innsbruck, which he shared with Best. Shortly afterwards five or six large buses arrived to take the *Prominenten* on the next step of their strange journey southwards.

Just as 'Wolf' and 'Fox'[2] moved into their buses, Mayer was called out to meet Gauleiter Hofer once again.

Accompanied by Primbs and Hans Boysen, his radio operator who had surrendered to the Germans, believing that nothing could happen to him now, Sergeant Mayer marched proudly past the assembled brownshirts waiting in the great hall of the Lachhof.

Hofer came out to meet them. 'The time has come,' he said, 'to act. I want to discuss with you how we can avoid a blood-letting in the Tyrol.'

'I've already made you my offer,' Mayer said. 'If you like, I can get US soldiers here to discuss terms.' With commendable energy which showed he had learned a lot from his adopted nation, he turned to Boysen and said, 'Let's see if we can get Bari.'

Hofer shook his head. 'It's too late for that. I've just learned that the American 103rd Division has crossed the frontier from Bavaria and is marching into the Tyrol. Their advance guard is already located on the Zirl Mountain.'

'All right,' Mayer said. 'I'll drive to Zirl and talk with our fellows.'

Hofer agreed in principle, but first of all he wanted to declare Innsbruck an open city and together they worked out the text of a radio address which Hofer broadcast a few hours later. But they had not reckoned with Kesselring, who

[2] The Gestapo code-names for Best and Stevens; both survived the war.

reacted angrily to the radio talk, stating that 'Your decision will not be recognized by my troops. I demand you come to Berchtesgaden for a discussion [of the problem] at once.'

Fearful to go himself, Hofer sent his assistant *Gauleiter*, who happened to be a corporal in the German Mountain Corps. It seemed almost as if the confused three-sided battle being fought in the mountain fastnesses of the Alpine Redoubt was being directed by NCOs. But he had no success with the Field-Marshal. He refused to surrender or to declare Innsbruck an open city.

Hofer decided to ignore Kesselring's threats. Placing himself in Mayer's hands, he allowed him to 'formally' intern him and gave Boysen the charge of a police guard to supervise the internment. Mayer then took Hofer's black Mercedes, its bonnet covered by a white sheet in token of surrender, and set off for the American lines. He managed to talk his way through the lines of the Herman Goering Division, convince the Commanding General of the 103rd to give him an officer to accompany him back through the Hermann Goering Division's positions and then stage-manage the surrender of Hofer's whole command as well as that of Austria's second city. This inspired the 05 'resistance' movement in Innsbruck to revolt. Under the command of Dr Karl Gruber, one day to be the Republic of Austria's foreign minister, they started to take over control of all important buildings and barracks. After some little blood-shed, they managed to calm the situation sufficiently to begin publication of post-war Austria's first newspaper *Die Tiroler Nachrichten*.

It came on the streets just as the first Americans of the 103rd Division began to march through Innsbruck on their way south. Printed on one side of the looted paper they had used was Hofer's last proclamation to his 'subjects': 'STICK IT OUT!' On the other, was Gruber's *cri-de-coeur:* 'THE MOMENT OF YOUR LIBERATION HAS COME AT LAST!' Neither had much effect. Within half-an-hour of their taking over Innsbruck's administration, the Americans had banned the *Tiroler Nachrichten*.

The capital of the Alpine Redoubt had fallen and the last

potential centre of German resistance was destroyed. The OSS had triumphed all along the line.[3] There was only one last secret for them to discover in Twelveland. *Where was Adolf Hitler?*

[3] While Sgt Mayer had been effecting the Tyrolean surrender, his boss Dulles had brought the negotiations for the surrender of the German armies in N. Italy to a successful conclusion.

PART FIVE

THE LAST OP.

(1945)

'Es geht alles vorueber.
Es geht alles vorbei.
Nach jedem Dezember,
Gibts wieder ein Mai.'

German popular song of 1945.

Everything passes.
Everything ends.
After every December,
There is always a May.

1

WHERE IS ADOLF HITLER?

Carl Johann Wiberg had been in business in Berlin for over thirty years, but in the spring of 1945, the middle-aged Swede had nothing to do. His glue factory, which had produced special metal adhesives, had been completely destroyed by the Allied air raids. All that seemed left to the 49-year-old widower—his wife had died in 1939—was to go walking with his pet dachshunds, *Onkel Otto* and *Tante Effi*.

Every morning he would prepare the two dogs on the second-floor balcony of his Wilmersdorf flat—for some reason, which his neighbours could not understand, he always had two ropes hanging from it—then dress himself carefully in his immaculate topcoat and Homburg before setting off with them through the bomb-shattered suburbs of Berlin. Occasionally he would break his morning walk to stop at his favourite corner bar on the Nestorstrasse, where he would listen to the latest gossip. It was usually pretty accurate too, for Harry Rosse's bar was favoured by the local National Socialist bigwigs and *Wehrmacht* officers on duty in the capital. Sometimes, too, he would patronize a special food shop which sold items without coupons to customers who were prepared to pay in foreign currency or at excessively high prices. Here, too, he kept his ears open.

His morning walk completed, Wiberg would return to his apartment, which was kept shuttered and barred, to receive his new fiancée, a Berlin girl named Inger, and instruct her yet once again what to do if the Gestapo came. 'Through the flat onto the back balcony and then down the ropes into the courtyard.' For Carl Wiberg was a spy, the OSS's resident agent in Nazi Berlin.

'Since I had lived over thirty years in Berlin and knew the old Germany, Hitler's acts after 1933 filled me with disgust,' Wiberg recalled.[1] 'The war that Hitler provoked was the last straw for me. I began to hope that something would happen to free humanity from the Nazi régime and its servants. In addition I had always felt the greatest admiration for the English and their democracy.'

Up to 1944 Wiberg's distaste for the Nazi régime had been confided solely to close Swedish friends. One such was a leather manufacturer whom he had known for twenty-five years. Just before the war this man had returned to Stockholm and set up in business there. In 1943 he met another man in the same trade, a Dane named Hennings Jessen-Schmidt. But Jessen-Schmidt was no ordinary businessman. He was also a leader of the Danish resistance and a member of the OSS.

After feeling the Swedish friend out, Jessen-Schmidt asked if he knew a reliable man in Berlin. The result was a cable to Wiberg saying that he was urgently needed in Stockholm. In September, 1944, he managed to get the necessary exit visa and a seat on a plane and so met the Dane for the first time.

They talked together for five hours and as Wiberg remembers today, 'I was both surprised and shocked. I realized immediately the risk I was running and knew what would happen to me in the hands of the Gestapo if anything went wrong. I asked for some time to think over his offer to work for him, though in reality I had already made up my own mind that I might be able to make some small contribution to the end of this terrible war in this manner.'

Before he left Stockholm that month he had agreed to become the OSS man in Berlin. It was his task to establish the 'mood of the German people and their reaction to the bombing as well as any governmental plans'. In addition, he was to be the OSS storekeeper in Berlin.

Thus Wiberg became the OSS's first man in Berlin and in the months that followed his apartment became a storehouse for the organization's deadly supplies. At night strange individuals would arrive at his door bearing cartons

[1] In a letter to the author.

'from your friends in Stockholm', as they would explain, and leave him with yet more weapons.

By the spring of 1945 Wiberg had a variety of drugs, poisons and knockout drops hidden throughout his flat. In the cellar and a garage he rented nearby, he kept a small arsenal of revolvers and rifles. The organization had even delivered a suitcase full of a highly volatile explosive, which worried him considerably, until he had found the perfect hiding place for it—in a strong box in the vault of the local branch of the Deutsche Union Bank!

All the same he could not help worrying about the danger of his flat being hit by an Allied bomb. What would happen if the police and local fire brigade started combing through his possessions? His fears were heightened that spring when one of the couriers from the OSS HQ in Stockholm actually delivered a supply of contraband goods during daylight and not at night during an air raid as had been agreed upon. Wiberg was furious with his boss Jessen-Schmidt, who had smuggled himself into Germany via Flensburg, hidden in a Danish fish truck. As he remarked later: 'Somebody had acted in a very naive and amateurish way and seemed bent on wrecking the entire operation.' It was with relief that he and Jessen-Schmidt learned from their couriers that the Anglo-American troops would enter Berlin in the middle of April.

But in the second week of that month, Wiberg received a shock. Jessen-Schmidt told him he had just heard from a courier that the Allies would not be attacking Berlin; the German capital would be left to the Russians. Unknown to the two OSS men, Allen Dulles' great intelligence coup, the discovery of the 'Alpine Redoubt', had changed the whole direction of Eisenhower's drive. Instead of Berlin being his main target, the emphasis had now been switched to the south.[2]

[2] In all fairness to Dulles, it must be pointed out that the discovery of the Redoubt came at a very convenient moment for Eisenhower. After the débâcle in the Ardennes and the role Montgomery had played in that battle, his two principal US commanders, Patton and Bradley, were in open revolt. If Berlin were the main objective, Montgomery in the north would gain the kudos of victory. If, on the other hand, the Redoubt were the main target, Bradley and Patton would win the

Then Wiberg had a stroke of luck. He was shopping in the special store when he heard a tremendous piece of news. Two well-dressed women, who he knew were the wives of high-ranking National Socialist officials, dropped a piece of information that he knew Colonel David Bruce back in London would receive with open arms. Although his face betrayed no emotion, Wiberg could feel his hands begin to tremble. A few minutes later he left the store and set out to find his boss.

Jessen-Schmidt was as excited as Wiberg when he heard the news. For several hours they discussed it from all angles and finally decided it must be accurate. As the radio transmitter in Wiberg's coal cellar was still not assembled, they had to wait until the Dane could find a courier to pass the information to London.

On the afternoon of Wednesday 12 April, the courier appeared and the news was on its way. It was simple but dramatic: Adolf Hitler had located his headquarters at the little town of Bernau some fourteen miles north-east of the city. What better birthday present could there be for the 'greatest commander of all ages', as Wiberg called him cynically, on 20 April,[3] than a large scale Allied bomber raid?

honours. In other words, personal reasons played a great role too in the change of strategy. See the author's *Bradley* (Ballantine Illustrated History of World War II) for further details.

[3] Hitler's last and sixty-fifth birthday.

2

THE LAST ATTEMPT

Adolf Hitler rose at eleven o'clock on the morning of his sixty-fifth birthday. Eva Braun, his mistress, presented him with a portrait of herself in a jewelled, silver frame. A short time later Hitler's 'brown eminence', Martin Bormann, made his daily appearance. By now Bormann, who was General Schellenberg's number one suspect as the Russians' source of information at the Führer's HQ was indispensable. He brought roses for the Führer.

Between eleven and twelve the inner clique all presented their regards—Speer, Doenitz, von Ribbentrop, Keitel, Jodl, Himmler.

Someone discovered an ancient gramophone and the birthday group played the only record they could find, a popular little movie tune of that year: *Blutrote Rosen erzaehlen dir vom Glueck*.[1] The title seemed very apt, for the sky that morning was dominated by the red of the Soviet artillery in the East.

Schellenberg heard the anti-aircraft fire as he was shaving. Just before he had gone to bed that morning he had toasted the Führer's health in champagne with Himmler. But as the day progressed he forgot the loyal toast. While the 88s hammered away at the British and Russian bombers he turned his attention to betraying his Führer along with the man whom Hitler had once called 'my loyal Heinrich'.

Himmler's face, when he returned from paying his respects to Hitler, was lined with worry and there were deep circles under his eyes. Schellenberg told him that he had

---

[1] Blood-red roses tell you of happiness.

received a telephone call from Count Folke Bernadotte, the cousin of Prince Carl Bernadotte, stating that if Himmler wanted him to act as a peace negotiator, Himmler must come to him before six o'clock the next morning. The Reichsführer nodded. He would leave Berlin and start the surrender negotiations.[2]

Before the meeting the Count said to Schellenberg, 'The Reichsführer no longer understands the realities of his own situation. I cannot help him any more. He should have taken Germany's affairs into his own hands after my first visit. I can hold out little chance for him now. And you, my dear Schellenberg, would be wiser to think of yourself.'

It was unnecessary advice. The young general was a born survivor. Soon he was to fly to Sweden, taking his dark secrets with him and leaving his masters to their fates. 'For the time being,' as he said much later, 'my services were not required.'[3]

Thus while the last surviving German spymaster in Berlin prepared to flee and his master celebrated his final birthday against the unholy background of a burning, dying Berlin, the two OSS agents Carl Wiberg and Hennings Jessen-Schmidt prepared to watch the assassination of the Führer at Bernau. Both dressed in elegant business suits, they crouched in the fields outside the little town and waited. They were not disappointed.

At 300 mph, twin-engined British bombers came winging in low and right on time. The 88s began to hammer away. But the RAF bombers were not to be deflected from their course. Time and again they roared down out of the April sky, and when they finally disappeared, leaving a burning town behind them, their place was taken by Russian *Stormovik* dive-bombers. As the two agents watched the

---

[2] The Allies at this time were putting great pressure on the Swedes to enter the war on their side. The Swedes, fearful of doing so, were trying to show their good will by offering to accept any concentration camp inmates the Germans would release. This was the reason for Count Bernadotte's mission to Germany.

[3] Much to his chagrin, Schellenberg's undoubted talents in the field of espionage were never required again. He died in exile in Italy in 1952, at the age of 42.

destruction of the little town as a direct result of their information, it was clear to them that Colonel Bruce had passed on the news of Hitler's presence to the Russians too.

One day later, however, they found out that all their efforts had been in vain. 'The British were there. The Russians were there. *The only person who wasn't present was Adolf Hitler!*'[4]

Like all the other attempts to kill the Führer over the twelve years, four months and seven days that the '1,000 Years Reich' lasted, this one ended in failure. But now it no longer mattered. Eleven days later, Adolf Hitler committed suicide in the 'Führer bunker'.

On the morning of that day, Wiberg and Jessen-Schmidt had identified themselves as OSS agents to a Red Army Colonel, standing outside Wiberg's house in Berlin-Wilmersdorf, when the Swede heard screams coming from the basement.

He broke off the conversation and rushed inside to find another Red Army officer trying to rape his fiancée, Inger Mueller. The girl's clothing was torn and the Russian's flies were open.

The Red Army Colonel, who had rushed after Wiberg, pulled out his pistol and whipped the would-be rapist across the face with it unmercifully. Frog-marching him outside into the rubble-littered streets and screaming '*Amerianski!*' all the time, he thrust the other Russian against the nearest wall and made ready to shoot him.

Wiberg dashed forward and thrust himself between the two. 'You can't just shoot a man like that!' he yelled.

In the end the Colonel relented and had the other man arrested. The would-be rapist was marched away to an unknown fate.

Thus, because of Dulles' mistaken interpretation of the intelligence coming out of the mythical 'Alpine Redoubt', the Red Army was allowed to enter Berlin first. Unwittingly too, the two members of his organization had their first clash with that other great super-power with which the

[4] Carl Wiberg in a letter to the author. Hitler was, of course, in his bunker in Berlin.

United States intended to divide up the post-war world. It would be the first of many such clashes to come in the months and years ahead. Already the new battle for Twelveland had begun.

AFTERMATH

'Those who were caught by the great illusion of
our time, and have lived through its intellectual
and moral debauch, either give themselves up to
a new addiction of the opposite type or are con-
demned to pay with a lifelong hangover.'

Arthur Koestler: The God That Failed.

One morning in late April, 1945, a young French soldier
guarding the Horber Bridge some thirty miles from the
German town of Stuttgart was startled to see a long column
of US vehicles approaching his position. He alerted his CO
and the two waited for the first jeep to pull up in front of
them.

A Colonel in the OSS jumped out, followed by his inter-
preter. The Colonel said he had come from General Devers.
commanding the US 7th Army, to congratulate the French
on their seizure of the bridge. He also had orders to push on
deeper into the heart of the Swabian hinterland.

Before the French officer had a chance to protest that the
area belonged to the French Army's area of operations the
colonel had jumped back into his jeep and was bouncing
across the bridge followed by his convoy, which contained
not only GIs but civilians and soldiers dressed in British
uniforms.

The Colonel's name was Boris Pash and he was a member
of the top secret Alsos operation. A 'Zorro in uniform', as
he has been described by one writer[1] he was a former Hollywood highschool teacher of athletics, whose sole claim to
pre-war fame was that he had 'discovered' the original
'sweater girl', Lana Turner. Since D-Day, however, he had
been searching Western Europe for a vastly different type of
'discovery'—Germany's atomic scientists. Now he was closer
than he had ever been to them. Their location had first

[1] Bar-Zohar: *La Chasse aux Savants Allemands* (Fayard).

217

been discovered in early 1944 when Moe Berg, once a famous baseball player and now one of Dulles' men in Berne, reported that one of them, Werner Heisenberg, lived near Hechingen in Southern Germany. Pash knew that the French would occupy Hechingen soon after they had taken Sigmaringen, where the Vichy Administration had found refuge. And Pash and his political masters did not want the French to capture those all-important German scientists.[2]

Accordingly when he was safely on the road to Hechingen he radioed back to the French, 'Keep out of the area of Hechingen. It is scheduled to be hit by an artillery bombardment in a few hours.' Naturally Pash had no intention of risking the lives of the German scientists by shelling Hechingen; his radio message was simply a ruse to keep the French in their positions for a little longer.

Thereafter the capture of Hechingen was a walkover. As soon as Pash had entered no-man's land, he began telephoning the first German-held village. He got through on the civilian telephone system and told the burgomaster he had better surrender—or else. The dodge worked and was repeated in every one of the villages which followed. On 23 April the Pash column entered Haigerloch, the site of the first experimental German atomic pile. One day later the Colonel drove into Hechingen.

A few hours later they were followed by French Colonial troops, but they were more interested in the local chickens and pigs than the German atomic scientists—Otto Hahn, Max von Laue, von Weizaecker—being busily rounded up by Pash for smuggling out of the future French Zone of Occupation.

The aptly named 'Operation Humbug' was an unqualified success.

Operation Humbug was typical of many such undercover OSS operations in Germany that month and in the weeks that followed. Atomic scientists, secret weapons, V-2s were stolen from the beaten Germans under the very noses of the

[2] The French attitude is exemplified by the fact that after they captured Stuttgart they refused to surrender it to the Americans to whose zone of occupation it was to belong. In the end General Eisenhower was forced to cut off supplies to the French Army and thus force them to give up the city.

other Allies; and not only from the French and Russians, but also the British, with whom the Alsos team worked in close co-operation.[3]

Yet the OSS bosses in Europe, Colonel David Bruce and Allen Dulles, were not concerned solely with the secret operation to plunder Twelveland of its scientific brains and military know-how. They were also worried about the role Russia would play in post-war Germany.

Already an OSS agent had been murdered by communist partisans in Italy after he had refused to hand over OSS funds to them.

The Russians were refusing to co-operate in the search for war criminals such as Martin Bormann, who was reputed to be alive, or to help in clearing up the mystery surrounding Hitler's fate in Berlin.[4] That summer, when Dulles took over OSS operations in Germany, it was clear to him from the reports coming from his agents that not only were the Russians attempting to communize their own zone of occupation but they were deliberately setting out to foment 'whispering campaigns' against the US in its zone 'on higher orders'.

From his headquarters in Weisbaden, Dulles, conservative by nature and a long-time associate of 'big business', decided that something ought to be done to counter the growing Soviet influence in the West. On 6 June, he ordered one of his associates, Swiss-born Mrs Emmy Rado, to drive Wilhelm Hoegner, formerly his adviser in Berne, to Bavaria. Hoegner, a socialist and fervent anti-communist, soon became Bavaria's first premier with Dulles's active support,

[3] In Nordhausen, captured by the Americans, but soon to be surrendered to the Russians, 100 intact V-2s were captured. They were smuggled out of Germany and loaded onto a convoy of ships at the British main port of supply, Antwerp. The SIS got wind of the operation, which was a breach of the agreement that such weapons would be examined and shared by both countries. The US convoy was stopped by the British Royal Navy in the North Sea and 50 V-2s demanded. The Americans refused and in spite of the diplomatic notes exchanged between the two Allies, all 100 finally landed in New Orleans to become the foundation of the US space and missile programme.

[4] See the author's *The Hunt for Martin Bormann* (Ballantine) for further details. In the end the SIS delegated Trevor-Roper to clear up the Hitler mystery.

founding a tradition which is exemplified to this day in the person of Franz Josef Strauss.

Under the code-name of 'Crown Jewels', Mrs Rado continued her operation, returning exiled German politicians of known anti-communist inclination to their homeland. In this way Erich Ollenhauer, who had spent the war in London, was brought back and eventually became the chairman of the West German Social Democratic Party.

At the same time Dulles's labour section under a former Washington labour attorney, Gerhard Van Arkel, tried to help re-establish the German Unions in the American Zone of Occupation in the hope that there would be no swing among their members towards the extreme left. There wasn't and the German Trade Union Association, under the long-time leadership of the former Jewish 'emigré' Rosenberg, was to play a great role in West Germany's political stability and financial recovery. But unknown to van Arkel and Dulles, the Russians already had a potential spy in the organization, Erica Glaser, who was van Arkel's secretary-interpreter.[5]

The 24-year-old daughter of a half-Jewish doctor who had fled from Germany after she had been beaten by boys of the Hitler Youth and a placard announcing 'I am a Jewish heathen' hung round her neck, had been 'adopted' by Dulles's Swiss associate, Noel Field. (Her parents finally landed in England where Erica's brother was shot down just before the end of the war while serving with the RAF.)

Now in the summer of 1945 she returned to her homeland under the auspices of the OSS, where she soon made contact with Leo Bauer, the long-time Comintern operative who had now been released from Swiss internment and had established himself in the state of Hesse. 'I was quite ready to tell him everything I knew about the OSS,' she recalled later. 'I told him that the OSS collected information about people all over Germany and that they had a certain control over

---

[5] There were others. Even before the war ended a Washington newspaper carried the alarmist headline 'House Unit Probe Reveals Red Link of OSS Official'. Fifteen years later, Hans Hirschfeld, then Willy Brandt's press aide and wartime OSS employee, was accused of being a wartime Soviet spy. He maintained that the accusation was an attempt to embarrass the Social Democratic Party.

the foundation of parties, the unions and newspapers[6] . . .
The Social Democrats were putting their people in the
unions and it seemed important to me that the communists
gained a good reputation in OSS circles and that they were
able to place their people in key positions.'

Although Bauer told her she should start spying on the
Americans, his comrades were not enthusiastic about her
offer; she suspected that they had other sources of information within the OSS. Still she was determined to supply the
Russians with material. On impulse she flew to Berlin in US
uniform, borrowed a jeep from a local motor pool of the US
Army there and drove to Karlshort in East Berlin, where
top German communists and their Russian masters planned
their political take-over of Germany behind high walls.

There she knocked on the door of Franz Dahlem, a communist recently released from Mauthausen concentration
camp, who was known to her through her adoptive 'father',
Noel Field. 'He was so scared to see me in American
uniform', she explained later, 'that he nearly fainted. He
kept running to the window and looking out and asking me
whether any Russian officer had seen me.'

Cynically Erica Glaser replied that of course she had
been seen by the Russians; how otherwise could she have
got into the compound? She then told him that she was
working for the OSS. 'I don't like the job especially, but all
the same I think it is useful for us. I am prepared to do
everything I can to help the Communist Party. Surely that's
of interest to you?'

Amazingly enough Dahlem refused her offer. He told her
she must obey the new Party rule that no communist could
work for the western occupation powers. In his opinion, she
should give up her job with the OSS, join the Party and obey
its rules.

Erica Glaser continued to argue a little longer, but in the
end she gave up. Sadly she left, got into her jeep and lifting
up the unguarded red-and-white barrier pole, as she had
done on entering, drove off into the night.

Nobody in the Russian camp seemed interested in Noel

[6] Ironically enough the OSS founded the *Neues Deutschland*, today
the organ of the East German communist state.

Field's tremendous offer. But the Russians had not heard the last of either Field or Erica Glaser.

When an unprecedented offer to spy on Russia came Dulles' way that summer, he seized it with both hands. In April, 1945, he had already learned from Wood that a group of German Army Intelligence men from the 'Foreign Armies East' Group, which had been the eyes and ears of the *Wehrmacht* in Russia since 1942, were prepared to offer their services to the Americans. In the confusion that followed Germany's surrender, Dulles lost sight of this group under its legendary commander, General Reinhard Gehlen.

When Gehlen and his men finally surrendered to the Americans in the Alpine Redoubt at a place aptly named *Elendsalm*—'Misery meadow'—they wanted nothing to do with him until a young American CIC sergeant named Victor de Guinzbourg interrogated him and forwarded his report to Colonel William Quinn, Chief-of-Intelligence to the US 7th Army. To him the name Gehlen rang a bell.

Quinn knew it well. He had met Dulles several times in 1944 and early 1945, when he had been alarmed enough by Dulles' reports to be taken in by the Alpine Redoubt. In due course he had contributed to the alarming SHAEF analysis of the threat which had led to the major change in US strategy in the closing months of the war. During those meetings with Dulles he had also heard of Gehlen and his supposed plan to leave behind an agent network in the territories to be occupied by the advancing Red Army.

Quinn ordered Gehlen to be brought to Augsburg and there he interrogated the man who was soon to provide eighty per cent of Nato's intelligence about the Russians. Satisfied by what he heard, Quinn passed the German General up the ladder until he reached General Sibert, Bradley's Chief-of-Intelligence, who had blundered badly in the previous December when he had failed to spot the signs indicating the German surprise attack in the Ardennes.

Sibert, a former West Point professor, did not share the Regular Army's disdain for the OSS. He knew Dulles well and had worked with him on a scheme in November, 1944, to get the German front line commanders in the Aachen area to capitulate. It had failed, but Sibert had retained his confidence in Dulles. Sibert decided that Gehlen's apparently unrivalled knowledge of the Red Army should not be lost to the US Army and ordered Gehlen to pick three of his best officers to accompany him to an unknown destination. Without Eisenhower's approval, but with that of his Chief-of-Staff, General Bedell Smith, soon to be head of the new CIA, they smuggled him out of Germany.

In Washington Gehlen was passed from office to office. Allen Dulles, who had just returned from Wiesbaden prior to retiring to his old pre-war job, was confident that the United States would be able to use him. Suddenly, however, a great crisis broke out in the OSS. Naval and Military Intelligence had long disliked the 'new boys', but they had been unable to do anything about it as long as Roosevelt lived.[7]

Thus by the end of the war General Strong, the head of Army Intelligence, was not talking to General Donovan and, according to Dr Lovell, Strong once shouted at him: 'Lovell, go back to Wildman Donovan and tell him that his amateur gang is going to be thrown out of the war effort entirely. I'm seeing the President on it and J. Edgar Hoover[8] is going with me!'

When, however, Roosevelt died, the new President, Harry Truman, who disliked both Donovan and the OSS because Roosevelt had never let him see the intelligence they supplied, was easily persuaded to disband the organization. In a brief order dated 20 September, 1945, he notified Donovan that the Office of Strategic Services would be terminated 'with effect from October 1st'. And his accompanying letter to Donovan was as curt and cold as the order. It read: 'I want to express my thanks for the capable leadership you have brought to the wartime activities of the OSS which will not be needed in time of peace.'

Thus in the autumn of 1945 the organization which had contributed so materially to the victory over Twelveland and had been the first official US agency to spot the new

[7] It took another nine months before Gehlen could start his well-known operation, due to the dissolution of the OSS.

[8] Head of the FBI and no friend of the OSS, or the SIS, which he suspected, rightly, of engineering the whole OSS business as a rival service to his own.

danger threatening that country, was wound up with un-ceremonious haste. Like a pack of jackals its rivals descended upon the still warm body to grab what they could.[9]

In London, too, Major-General Sir Stewart Menzies was paying off old scores that summer. Group-Captain Winter-botham[10] the man who had invented 'scientific intelligence' went without a pension. For a short time he was on the board of BOAC, but that job didn't last long; the intrigue there was as bad as in the SIS headquarters and soon he was back to where he had started in 1929 when he had dug him-self out of his snow-bound rundown farm to go down to London to join the SIS. With 'literally threepence'[11] in his pocket, he began life once again in a remote Devonshire village, where his newly acquired farmhouse did not even possess a roof.

Commander Denniston went too. He was awarded the CMG and a pension of £591 a year, poor recompense for what he had done for his country and the status of the SIS. At sixty-three, he too had to begin all over again and return to the teaching job he had left in 1914, teaching Latin and French at a boys' school at Epsom. When he died sixteen years later, not one word of his great contribution to the war was ever made public. He died unknown, but perhaps that would have been the way he would have liked it.

Soon Colonel Sir Claude Dansey would go too, to die two years later in Bath.

But other, more deadly scores were being paid off that summer. At Lachtmere House, a three-storey manor house,

[9] It was obvious that powerful men were gunning for Donovan as early as February, 1945, when his top-secret report suggesting to Roose-velt that the USA needed a post-war intelligence service was 'leaked' to the press. Tht *Chicago Tribune* wrote, for example, that the plan de-manded 'prompt congressional denunciation of the adoption of Gestapo, Nazi secret police and OGPU Russian secret police methods in the United States'. Donovan never found out who 'leaked' the information about the scheme. My guess is either Hoover or Dulles, whom Donovan had rejected for a top job in the OSS, and who would be soon the architect of its successor the CIA.

[10] The rank was 'borrowed' in order to be able to deal with the brass during the Second World War.

[11] Conversation with author.

hidden behind a high wall in the Surrey village of Ham Common, Menzies' ex-enemies in the *Abwehr* were assembled for interrogation—and sentence.

Under the command of a bemonocled Rhodesian colonel nick-named 'Tin-eye' Stephens, a skilled staff put the Germans and their former agents through their paces. Giskes was there and 'Freddy', the star of Twelveland's counter-espionage section's last agent.[12] Hooper was there too.

Colonel Giskes was subjected to harsh and often humiliating treatment there, being brought from the centre's 'cage' —it's still there—to the manor house itself where he was stripped naked and faced with hour-long interrogation by relays of SIS men. He was prepared to discuss his role in Operation North Pole which had resulted in the capture and death of some 42 SOE agents in Holland; but that was all. One day, however, he heard a voice that he had last heard at the *Hotel Dom* in Cologne six years before. Risking a glance over the balcony at the courtyard below, he recognized its owner at once, although he was sporting a captain's 'pips' and the khaki of the British Army. It was Hooper!

Years later he recalled: 'I was not prepared to betray anyone. But Hooper was different. I was still angry with him. Six years before, he'd tried to murder me.'

In October, 1939, he had received an urgent message from Hooper in the Hague asking him to come from Hamburg as he had something for him which he could only give him in person. Giskes took the next train to Holland. At Enschede on the German-Dutch border, while the train was stopped at customs, a frantic official thrust a 'train telegram' into his surprised hands. It was from his chief in Hamburg. It had been discovered that Hooper was working for the British again and, together with Major Stevens, he had cooked up a scheme to lure Giskes to Holland where 'undoubtedly he would have plunged me into the nearest *graacht* to keep me silent for good'.[13]

The next time his British interrogator ran him through

---

[12] Freddy, the Austrian who had 'penetrated' the Churchill family, disappeared suddenly in June, 1945, after several mysterious trips in a huge black limousine never to be seen at Ham Common again.
[13] In a conversation with the author.

his paces about the events leading to the Venlo Incident which had come as such a tremendous shock to Menzies, Giskes admitted to him that it had been him and not his colleague Captain von Feldmann who had made the initial contact. Von Feldmann had really been in Portugal at the time and not in Germany as he had told his interrogator up to then. He also revealed his contact within the Continental SIS. Immediately, he was taken out to identify Hooper who was strolling around with a group of khaki-clad soldiers in the courtyard. He did so and was dismissed.

A month later when he was brought to the main house for questioning again, he asked his interrogator what had happened to Hooper.

The answer was a laconic 'We've hanged him!'

The wheel had come full circle; after six long years Hooper, the arch-traitor, had been betrayed himself.

But if Menzies did do a little house-cleaning in that summer of victory, while in Washington its indirect creation the OSS stumbled, fell and finally died altogether, his Secret Intelligence Service remained essentially what it had been when he had taken over its command in 1939. Like so many British institutions at the end of the Second World War, it rested on its laurels, as if somehow drained of energy, content solely with congratulating itself on the 'great job of work' it had done.

Yet any superficial examination of the role the two services—the SIS and the OSS—had played in the battle for Twelveland would have shown that the latter organization had gained its successes by having active agents within Germany—Wood, Erickson, Wiberg etc. The SIS's role, on the other hand, had been passive. As we have seen its successes were greater than those of the OSS, but they were based on passive intelligence: interrogation of German POWs, information smuggled out of Twelveland from untrained foreign forced labourers, and above all on the Bletchley operation.

But in the new struggle with a new enemy, signalled by the defection of the Russian cipher clerk Gouzenko that autumn in Canada,[14] there were no prisoners to be questioned, no

[14] Later it was shown that there were links between the Russian spy-

226

reports smuggled out by friendly foreign workers and their resistance movements and no enigma to betray the enemy's most intimate secrets.

Thus the SIS entered the new struggle for Twelveland and its neighbours in central Europe—now almost completely under Russian domination—as blind as it had entered the old one in 1939; and with the added disadvantage that the Russians had a spy in a key position among its ranks, Kim Philby who was obviously being groomed to become 'C' himself one day. 'If they hadn't caught up with Kim,' his fellow defector Maclean told his third wife in 1964, 'you'd be Lady Philby by now.' A communist head of the Secret Intelligence Service! A mind-boggling thought.

The Americans were little better prepared for the new struggle. On the basis of a memorandum put forward by Allen Dulles,[15] a successor to the disbanded OSS had been formed, the Central Intelligence Agency. But it had its growing pains.

The job of making America aware of the 'red threat' was left to Hoover's FBI and an assorted batch of politicians out to make a name for themselves (including a young hopeful from California named Richard Nixon). And they didn't do too good a job of it. Just as they got on to Hiss through Whittaker Chambers, a former Soviet agent in the USA, one of their key witnesses was found dead in suspicious circumstances. Laurence Duggan, who already had been questioned by the FBI but was scheduled for further interrogation, jumped or was pushed to his death from his sixteenth floor office in Fifth Avenue on a snowy night in

ring in wartime North America and the Dora network in Switzerland. Whether this information was 'planted'—perhaps with Foote's aid—is unknown.

[15] Just before his death General Donovan told Dr Lovell: 'The other day Allen Dulles came in here and said that President Truman had offered him the job [head of the CIA]. What did I advise? I told him, 'Allen, you were a great performer as a long operator, but Al, this CIA job needs an expert organizer and you're no good whatever at that ... He left damned upset at me, but God help America if he heads up CIA. It's like making a marvellous telegraph operator the head of Western Union!'

December, 1948. One of the men, he, as well as Chambers, had already named as being a Soviet spy was Dulles's old OSS associate Noel Field.

But Field was in Europe and left untouched. Six months later, out of a job and nearly broke, Noel Field took an Air France machine from Paris to Prague, where he booked into the Hotel Palace. Thereafter he disappeared. His wife followed him and also vanished. Then his brother Hermann disappeared too. Finally Erica Glaser, his 'daughter', took the same route east. Only Erica[16] came back.

But why had Field gone? Who had called him eastwards? Or had he been sent? And if he had been sent, who had done the sending? A lot of questions with few answers.

But in the months that followed Field was used by one central European government after another to purge itself of 'western spies, Tito deviationists, Zionist traitors'—indeed anyone in power in the new communist states, who Stalin thought would not toe the Moscow hard line. Rajk of Budapest went in 1949. The Hungarian Foreign Minister had known Field during the war in France. In the case against him and Dr Tibor Szoenyi, Field was described as the 'head of the US Secret Service under his chief Allen Dulles of the OSS... Field was a specialist in recruiting agents among so-called left wingers and various spy networks made up of emigrants of different nationalities in Switzerland were under his command.' The link with Field cost Laslo Rajk his head.

Ladislav Gomulka in Poland followed; then Trailscho Kostoff in Sofia and Leo Bauer in East Berlin.[17] But it was in Czechoslovakia, which had only been in communist hands for two years, that Noel Field played his greatest role. in 1950, 169,544 communists, one tenth of the Czech Communist Party, were thrown out of the Party because, as Vaclav Kopecky, the Czech Minister of Information, pointed out: 'Let us not forget that an international network of

[16] Her married name was Wallach, acquired after she had married and ex-GI who decided to stay and study in Europe.

[17] Both Leo Bauer and Erica Glaser were sentenced to death. After Stalin's death, Bauer's sentence was reduced to imprisonment. Finally he was freed and made his way to West Germany where he became Willy Brandt's senior adviser.

Anglo-American espionage has been discovered in connection with the well-known Noel Field.' One year later the man who had carried out that radical piece of Party surgery, Rudolf Slansky, was himself arrested; and with him a whole group of senior communist leaders who had had 'treacherous links' with Noel Field, his brother Hermann and that 'other agent of the British Secret Service', Conni Zilliacus, the left-wing British MP.

As a result of the notorious Slansky Trial and whole-scale purge of the Czech Communist Party new men came to the top, faceless men who would obey orders from Moscow without question. In 1953, Antonin Novotny, one-time *Kapo* from Mauthausen Concentration Camp, became the First Secretary of the Czech Communist Party.

In the wave of de-Stalinization that followed Khrushchev's famous speech to the 22nd Congress of the Soviet Communist Party, Novotny ordered an old comrade, Rudolf Barak, to look into the 1952 trials. But Barak had ideas of his own. He sent a detailed memorandum to Khrushchev listing the areas in which he suggested changes should take place in Czechoslovakia; and if Novotny was not prepared to take action, he, Barak, was. Besides, he let it be known in his own circle at the Ministry of the Interior that he knew some unpleasant things about Novotny's activities during his stay in Mauthausen Concentration Camp.

By 1962, Novotny who was also now President of the Czech State, felt it was time to act against his Minister of the Interior, who was head of the Secret Service as well as the ordinary police. He was tried, found guilty and given fifteen years' imprisonment.[18] During the resultant search of his ministry a safe was found to which apparently there was no key. The lieutenant-colonel in charge of the investigation of the Barak 'plot' had it forced open and found it crammed full of personal interrogations by Barak of wartime acquaintances of Novotny, in particular, of a man long thought dead, Commissar Nachtmann, the NKVD agent who had worked for the Gestapo.

When Novotny was shown the papers, he was said to have

[18] Dubcek had him released in 1968. Today, he is reported to be running a filling station.

229

suffered a mild heart attack. Recovering, he ordered Lubo-mir Strougal, once Minister of Agriculture, now the new Minister of the Interior, to lay this ghost from the past.

Nachtmann, who had been sent to Prague on Barak's request by Khrushchev, swiftly disappeared behind bars and Strougal's investigators spread out through the land in search of Barak's ghosts from the old war against Twelve-land. In a remote provincial prison they discovered a strange prisoner: a small shaven-headed German of fifty or so who had special privileges and a direct line to Barak himself. A Major Benes questioned him, but could get nothing out of him. The case was referred to Strougal and he called in Colonel Miller, the head of the Czech Secret Service.[19]

Miller saw the way the wind was blowing. He told Strougal the full story of the mysterious German prisoner, who up to now had refused to give his name. He had been found four years before in Argentina, where he had been kid-napped and smuggled aboard a Czech ship bound for Stettin. From there he had been transported to Prague by car, where Barak had questioned him about Novotny's activities as a 'Gestapo agent' in Mauthausen Concentration Camp be-tween 1941 and 1945.

The strange German prisoner was the same 'decent little man' who had once questioned Stevens and Best so long before—'*Gestapo Mueller!*'[20]

The number of the survivors of the great secret battle in Twelveland was growing smaller.

In 1951, the CIA decided that Kim Philby, SIS's repre-sentative in Washington, was a Russian spy and that it was he who had tipped off Burgess and Maclean. General Bedell Smith, once Eisenhower's Chief-of-Staff and now head of the CIA, wrote Sir Stewart Menzies an angry letter making it clear that Philby had to leave the United States.

[19] Apparently he had worked for Russian Intelligence in Moscow until the era of de-Stalinization when he had been kicked out of his post and been forced to find employment elsewhere. If he is still alive today, he must undoubtedly still be behind bars as a man who knows too much and has sent too many to their deaths, including the British SOE agent he betrayed—24-year-old Mrs Oostinga.

[20] Strougal's Ministry launched a story at that time that Mueller had been spotted working in Albania as secret police adviser to the dictator. Whereafter he disappeared for good.

Sir Percy Sillitoe, the publicity-conscious chief of the MI5, flew to Washington to confer with Hoover, Bedell Smith and Dulles. The Philby case was, as Sillitoe remarked, 'a real shocker'. But the fact that the Americans had pointed the finger of suspicion at one of his key men and had been supported by the equally disdained MI5, only made Menzies more convinced that Philby was being victimized.

In June that year when Philby came home, he was received by Menzies, not as a culprit but as a man who had been hard done by by amateurs such as Hoover and Dulles, who knew nothing of the real intelligence work. And Philby helped to reinforce Menzies' confidence in him right from the start.

He told Menzies at their first interview: 'I'm no good to you now. I'll put in my resignation. I think you'd better let me go.'

Menzies was inclined to keep him but the pressure was on from both the Foreign Office and MI5; and Bedell Smith had sent C an ultimatum of great bluntness: 'Fire Philby,' he had written, 'or we break off the intelligence relationship.' It was one that Menzies could no longer ignore, in spite of the anti-Americanism of much of Britain's establishment at that time. The Secret Intelligence Service was now the junior partner of the service it had once helped to create.

As one of the last official acts before his retirement he allowed Philby to resign instead of firing him. Thus, unsung and unrecorded, the two of them passed from the corridors of power. Philby 'went out into the cold' for the next few years while Sir Stewart Menzies and his third and last wife, Audrey, retired to his tapestry-hung Elizabethan house near Chippenham in Wiltshire.

Another C came and went. For the first time in the SIS's history, a non-military man took over command, a member of the hated MI5, and a university graduate to boot. 'Colonel Dansey must be turning in his grave,' old SIS hands commented sadly. And the new C, Richard White, was convinced of Philby's guilt. But as yet he was biding his time. Philby was sent out to Beirut under the cover of a journalist working for the *Observer*; but, in reality, he was again an agent of the 'old firm'.

The treachery which Kim Philby had begun in July 1940, finally caught up with him twenty-three years later. On 1 January, 1963, his nerve cracked under the effect of the SIS suspicions. After an all-day party, which turned into a drunken orgy, he cracked his head on the radiator in his own bathroom. He was immediately hospitalized.

The new SIS resident in the local British Embassy asked Philby to call. But Philby now knew the British were on to him. Desperately he spun out his convalescence, waiting for the signal from his Russian masters that it would be safe for him to escape.

It came on 23 January, 1963. On the evening of that day, he disappeared into the darkness, never to be seen in the West again. Back in Britain the storm burst over the head of his old chief 'whom he would always remember with affection' (as Philby wrote hypocritically). Sir Stewart Menzies was broken by it. Thereafter, he began, 'to lose his health and his zest for life'. The great betrayal had wounded him mortally. In 1967 he had a hunting accident. He did not ride again.

On 6 June, 1968, the 24th anniversary of that great landing in France which he had helped to make possible, his 'zest for life' finally left him. The old Battle for Twelveland had claimed its last victim.

INDEX

Abendschoen, Willie, 69
Abetz, Otto, 122
Abwehr (German Secret Service), xi, xiii, xiv, 5, 6n, 7, 8, 10, 11, 12, 20n, 31, 32, 55, 56, 57, 64, 66, 70, 72, 75, 80, 81, 97, 99, 101, 115, 118, 133, 160n, 168, 184, 225
Agent A54, 62–6, 68, 69, 71
Agent 110, xiii, 110, 114, *see also* Dulles, Allen
'Agnes' (Ernst Lemmer), 85, 86, 87n
Air raids on London, 47
Air reconnaissance, 15–18, 20–1
Alpine Redoubt, 193–4, 197, 202–4, 211, 215, 222
Alsos operation, 217, 219
'Anna' (German informant), 90, 102
Anthropoid, 71, 72
'Athos' (radio receiver), 149
Atomic bomb research, 137–8, 140n
Atomic scientists, search for, 217–218
Attlee, Clement R., 152
Austria, resistance in, 193, 194, 204

Babington-Smith, Constance, 13n, 18, 162
Baldegg, Mayr von, 92
Ball-bearing industry, 169
Barak, Rudolf, 229, 230
Battle of Britain, 47
Bauer, Leo, 117, 118n, 220, 221, 228
Beaverbrook, Lord, 152
Becu, Omer, 190
Behn, Colonel, 168
Behrisch, Arno, 55, 56
Belgian resistance, 150
Benes, Major, 230
Beneš, President Eduard, 66, 71
Benson, Sir Rex, 23n

Berchtesgaden, and pornographic literature, 113
Berg, Moe, 218
Bernadotte, Count Folke, 214
Bernadotte, Prince Carl, 59, 60, 172–3, 177–8, 214
Best, Captain Payne, 31, 34–8, 65, 69, 70, 80, 201, 202–3, 203n, 230
Biggs, Ernest, 52, 56
Birnbaum, Immanuel, 54, 55
Bismarck, 57, 131
Bjoernstierna, Colonel, 57
Bletchley decoding operation, 44, 45, 46–7, 66, 99, 100, 104, 118, 131, 133, 186, 226
Blizna, Poland, 154, 156–8, 161
Blun, Georges, 85n
Boesendorfer, Esther, 84
Bohle, Ernst, 189
Bolli, Margit, 91–3
Boris, Czar, 103
Bormann, Martin, 69, 192, 213, 219
Boyle (SIS employee), 24
Boysen, Hans, 194, 203–4
Bradley, General Omar, 211n, 222
Brandt, Willy, xii, 52n, 86n, 118n, 220n, 228n
Braun, Eva, 182, 213
Breitner, Jochen, 64, *see also* Agent A54
Broglie, Jacqueline de, 183–4
Brown, Doctor, 122–3, 127, 128
Bruce, Colonel David, 113, 138, 179, 212, 215, 219
Bruneval raid, 142
'Buero Ha' (Swiss intelligence organization), 82, 93
Bulgaria, 103
'Bull, Mr' (Dulles, Allen *q.v.*), xiii, 109–14
Bupo, Swiss Federal Police, 92–3
Burgess, Alan, qu., 72
Burgess, Guy, 28, 230

233